The Beginner's Guide to Spiritual Gifts

The Beginner's Guide to Spiritual Gifts

SAM STORMS

VINE
BOOKS

SERVANT PUBLICATIONS
ANN ARBOR, MICHIGAN

Vine Books is an imprint of Servant Publications especially designed to serve
evangelical Christians.

Although the men and women whose stories are told in this book are real, many
of their names have been changed to protect their privacy.

Published by Servant Publications
P.O. Box 8617
Ann Arbor, Michigan 48107

Cover design by Alan Furst, Minneapolis, Minn.

02 03 04 05 10 9 8 7 6 5 4 3 2 1

Printed in the United States of America
ISBN 1-56955-311-4

Library of Congress Cataloging-in-Publication Data

Storms, Sam.
    The beginner's guide to spiritual gifts / Sam Storms.
        p. cm.
    Includes bibliographical references.
    ISBN 1-56955-311-4 (alk. paper)
    1. Gifts, Spiritual. I. Title.
    BT767.3 .S76 2002
    234'.13--dc21

                                                                2001007848

Joyfully dedicated to:

Jack Deere

for whose friendship, encouragement,
and insight I will forever be grateful

and

John and Jan Bingaman

whose love and support
continue to amaze me
and whose faithfulness in the joy of ministry
has been an indescribable blessing to me
and countless others

(I love you guys!)

Contents

ONE

When Power Comes to Church

I'm encouraged by some things I see in the church today. Attendance is up. So is giving, generally speaking. Conferences abound. Sales of books about the Bible and spirituality are soaring. Small groups continue to flourish. The winds of worship are blowing with increasing fervor. Christians, by and large, are becoming more active in the public arena and more vocal with their beliefs. So, yes, there are things that encourage me.

But then I look deeper, beyond the facade of religiosity, the flurry of activity, and the new $25 million sanctuary with padded pews. What I see is a gap—often a chasm—between what the church is and what it ought to be. I see the disparity between what Christians say and what they do, between what they know and how they live, between what they promise and how much they fulfill.

Preachers teach the Bible, and people snore. Homemakers share their faith, and it falls on deaf ears. Lives are broken and rarely get fixed. Bodies are suffering, and few are healed. Marriages are dying, and people just give up. Temptations are faced, and sin flourishes. The poor are hungry and stay that way.

I don't mean to sound overly pessimistic. There are some who think we're doing fine, but most of the people I know concede the church's lamentable impact on the spirituality of its members and its minimal influence on society at large. So, what's wrong?

It seems as if everyone has an opinion, and mine may be just one more in a seemingly endless list. But I'm convinced the problem is *power*, or, should I say, the *absence* of it.

Where I'm Coming From

My experience in church life is a bit unusual. I was raised as a Southern Baptist and never attended another church until I went to seminary in 1973. For three years I served as interim pastor of a Presbyterian church, not an easy thing for a Baptist to do! I spent sixteen years in two independent Bible churches and another seven in a Vineyard congregation. I now teach theology at one of America's premier Christian liberal arts colleges and have been attending a charismatic Anglican fellowship for the last year. I'm now at the point where my suspicions about what's wrong with the church in general have hardened into solid convictions.

My conclusion is this: The real problems, the painful struggles, and our diminishing impact won't be solved short of a fresh infusion of power—not just any power, mind you, but spiritual power, the kind of power that human flesh can't produce and education can't conceive and revamped programs can't strategize. The church desperately needs the power of her Lord and the energy and activity of the Holy Spirit.

As cynical as I may have sounded until now, I'm actually hopeful. For I have read the Book of Acts and see operative in the lives of those early believers something that I believe is no less available to us today. There is something that links us to the success of the early church and holds forth hope that we can and will emerge from our spiritual lethargy. There is something that can transform good intentions into life-changing actions and abstract theologizing into concrete impact.

I'm talking about spiritual gifts. Spiritual gifts, or the *charismata*, are God's answer to the human question: "Why can't *we* do that?" They are the manifestation and power of God the Holy Spirit through which he intends to lead the church into the fullness of its ordained end.

I know I risk being misunderstood. More than a few would point not to the lack of power, but to the abysmal theological immaturity in the church as the source of its struggle. I can't argue with that. Biblical illiteracy and theological naiveté have reached epidemic proportions in the church today. But more than knowledge is needed. Mere doctrine won't suffice. What the church needs is truth set aflame by the power of the Holy Spirit. What the church needs is the divine energy of God himself bringing what we know to bear on how we live and how we pray and how we love and how we witness. And let's not forget that *teaching* is itself a spiritual gift, no less a manifestation of the power of the Spirit than tongues or miracles! (See Rom. 12:7, 1 Cor. 12:29, Eph. 4:11).

The Ceasing of Cessationism

There was a time when I could not have written this book. For the first fifteen years of my ministry, I was a cessationist. This term refers to someone who believes the so-called miraculous gifts of the Holy Spirit ceased in the first century. The alleged cessation of such gifts as prophecy, speaking in tongues, healing, miracles, word of wisdom, word of knowledge, and the discerning of spirits is a view embraced by many in the evangelical community.

It's important for you to know that I didn't reject cessationism because I witnessed a miracle (although some who knew me at the time would insist my theological shift was itself a miracle!). I rejected cessationism because, in the solitude and safety of my office, I became convinced the Bible didn't teach it. It isn't the purpose of this book to describe my personal theological journey, nor to provide a defense of the contemporary validity of all

God's spiritual gifts. There are a number of books that do an admirable job, if that is what you need.[1]

Permit me, however, to share one critical insight. Perhaps the most painful part of this particular theological shift was my discovery of the primary reason I had so long resisted the full range of the Spirit's gifts. Beyond the biblical arguments to which I appealed, I was, quite frankly, embarrassed by the appearance and behavior of many in the public eye who were associated with spiritual gifts. I didn't like the way they dressed. I didn't like the way they spoke. I was offended by their lack of sophistication and their overbearing flamboyance. I was disturbed by their flippant disregard for theological precision and their excessive displays of emotional exuberance.

My opposition to spiritual gifts was also energized by fear— the fear of emotionalism; the fear of fanaticism; the fear of the unfamiliar; the fear of rejection by those whose respect I cherished and whose friendship I did not want to forfeit; the fear of what might occur were I fully to relinquish control of my life and mind and emotions to the Holy Spirit; the fear of losing what little status in the evangelical community my hard work had attained.

I'm talking about the kind of fear that energized a personal agenda to distance myself from anything that potentially linked me with people who, I believed, were an embarrassment to the cause of Christ. I was faithful to the eleventh commandment of Bible-church evangelicalism: "Thou shalt not do at all what others do poorly." In my pride I had allowed certain extremists to exercise more of an influence on the shape of my ministry than I did the text of Scripture. Fear of being labeled or linked or in some way associated with the "unlearned" and "unattractive" elements in contemporary Christendom exercised an insidious power on my ability and willingness to be objective in the reading of Holy Scripture. I am not so naive to think that my understanding of Scripture is now free from subjective influences! But I am confident that at least fear, in this form, no longer plays a part.

By the way, if all this sounds like the arrogance and self-righteousness of someone who prized "being right" above everything else, that's precisely what it was.

God *and* His Gifts, or God *in* His Gifts?

There's a crucial principle we need to understand from the outset: Spiritual gifts are not God bestowing to his people something external to himself. They are not some tangible "stuff" or substance separable from God. *Spiritual gifts are nothing less than God himself in us*, energizing our souls, imparting revelation to our minds, infusing power in our wills, and working his sovereign and gracious purposes through us. Spiritual gifts must never be viewed deistically, as if a God "out there" has sent some "thing" to us "down here." Spiritual gifts are God present in, with, and through human thoughts, human deeds, human words, human love.

The language Paul uses to make this point is explicit and often repetitive. Since this book is primarily concerned with the gifts listed in 1 Corinthians 12:4-11, let's look at this paragraph with a focus on what the apostle says concerning the origin or source or operative energy of the charismata. As you read, take special note of the italicized type.

Now there are varieties of gifts, but *the same Spirit*. And there are varieties of ministries, and *the same Lord*. And there are varieties of effects, but *the same God who works all*

things in all persons. But to each one is given *the manifestation of the Spirit* for the common good. For to one is given
the word of wisdom *through the Spirit,* and to another the
word of knowledge *according to the same Spirit;* to another
faith *by the same Spirit,* and to another gifts of healing *by
the one Spirit,* and to another the effecting of miracles, and
to another prophecy, and to another the distinguishing of
spirits, to another various kinds of tongues, and to another
the interpretation of tongues. But *one and the same Spirit
works all these things, distributing to each one individually
just as He wills.*

1 CORINTHIANS 12:4-11

For a fuller understanding of what Paul said, let's look at the
word translated "manifestation" *(phanerōsis)* in verse 7. This is
Paul's way of saying that the Spirit is himself made manifest or
visibly evident in our midst whenever the gifts are in use.
Spiritual gifts are concrete disclosures of *divine* activity and only
secondarily *human* activity. Spiritual gifts are the presence of the
Spirit himself coming to relatively clear, even dramatic, expression in the way we do ministry. Gifts are God going public
among his people.

To reject spiritual gifts, to turn from this immediate and
gracious divine enabling, is, in a sense, to turn from God. It's
no small issue whether one affirms or denies these manifestations of the divine presence. In affirming them, we welcome
him. In denying them, we deny him. This may sound harsh;
however, I'm not suggesting that cessationists *consciously* intend
to resist God's activity. But *resistance is the practical effect of
their theology, conscious or not.*

Whether spiritual gifts are for today is not some secondary, tangential issue that exists only for theologians to debate. It directly touches the very mission of the church and how she lives out her calling. How we speak to the world, the way we encounter the enemy, the expectations with which we minister to the broken and wounded and despairing are bound up in how we answer the question: Shall we or shall we not be the church of the Bible? Shall we or shall we not build the church with the tools God has provided?

I should make two additional qualifications. First, I would never suggest that the power of God is found only in spiritual gifts. God's power is operative in any number of ways and through a variety of means. The Spirit is no less responsible for joy, peace, and hope (Rom. 15:13) than he is for "signs and wonders" (Rom. 15:19). But there's no escaping the fact that the charismata described in the New Testament are the primary conduit through which divine energy enters our existence and empowers our otherwise listless lives and brings the church into the fullness of the knowledge and experience of Jesus Christ.

Second, not all cessationists (or even the majority) deny the possibility of miraculous phenomena occurring subsequent to the death of the apostles. What most cessationists deny is the post-apostolic operation of what they call "revelatory gifts" (prophecy, tongues, interpretation of tongues; although neither tongues nor interpretation are revelatory) and in particular the gift of "miracles" mentioned by Paul in 1 Corinthians 12:10. Whereas the potential for miracles is affirmed by most cessationists (but with minimal expectancy), the presence of the gift itself in contemporary church life is denied.

Similarly, most cessationists believe God can and occasionally does supernaturally heal people today. But they say the "gift" of healing is no longer available to the church. One of the principal reasons for this doctrine is a misconception about miraculous gifts. Many cessationists erroneously believe that a person who has "the gift of healing" or "the gift of miracles" must be able to invariably exercise supernatural power at will, on any occasion, at any time, with the same degree of success as did the apostles. When they measure this against what they perceive to be the infrequency and inefficiency of modern claims to the miraculous, it seems only reasonable to conclude that such charismata are no longer operative in the church. This is a point that I will take up in more detail later on.[2]

You're going to read a lot in this book about miraculous phenomena. When I use that terminology I don't mean the mere *potential* for rare supernatural activity or some surprising act of divine providence. I have in mind the *actual operation* of those miraculous gifts listed in 1 Corinthians 12:7-10, all of which, I believe, are available to the church today.

Why the "Nine" and Not All?

But why focus only on the gifts listed in 1 Corinthians 12:7-10? The answer is *not* because the other gifts are less important to the life of the church. There are three reasons I have chosen to focus our attention on the nine gifts in 1 Corinthians 12 (word of wisdom, word of knowledge, faith, healing, miracles, prophecy, distinguishing of spirits, tongues, interpretation of tongues).

First of all, the nature of these nine gifts is less obvious than the others. Mercy (Rom. 12:8), teaching (Rom. 12:7), exhortation (Rom. 12:8), and similar gifts are easier to understand and thus don't require as extensive an explanation as do the nine.

Second, these nine gifts are, for better or worse, extremely controversial. Sad to say, rather than uniting Christians in a concerted effort to build up the church, they have become the foil of many a divisive debate or church split. My aim is to shed light on these gifts; to clear away any theological fog; and to eliminate (or at least minimize) the caricatures that many in the church have, not only of these gifts, but also of the people who practice them.

Third, and finally, the church desperately needs an infusion of the supernatural activity of God into its life and ministry. Whereas all spiritual gifts require the energizing presence of "the same God" (1 Cor. 12:6), these nine are by nature more overt and powerful, at least in terms of their visible and vocal impact. I'm not advocating a sensationalistic approach to Christianity, nor do I believe that a person with the gift of prophecy, for example, is more essential (or more spiritual) than a person with the gift of teaching or leadership or mercy. But the church is woefully short of the life-changing, Christ-honoring power of the supernatural activity of the Spirit. Knowing that such gifts are available and understanding how they function is essential if the ills of the church are ever to be overcome.

So, here's why I've written this book. I want you to be *educated* about spiritual gifts. It's unlikely you'll be concerned about what you don't understand. Worse still, if the understanding you have is distorted or misinformed, your lack of concern can turn to outright opposition.

I also want you to be *equipped* to use the gifts God gives. Knowing what the gifts are is only half the story. We have to possess the practical wisdom, the spiritual skill, in knowing how and when and for whom the gifts are designed to operate.

Lastly, I want you to be *expectant* about what God can do for you and for those he's called you to help with his power. I want your faith and confidence in both God's goodness and his greatness to grow and intensify. Skeptics about what God can and will do rarely experience his power.

That's why I've written this book. That's why I hope you'll read it.

TWO

Right? Wrong!

Wonderful things in the Bible we see, things that are put there by you and by me!

I don't remember when I first heard those words, or even who said them, but at no time are they more true than when people talk about spiritual gifts. There are so many myths and misconceptions, I hardly know where to begin. But before I do, let's define spiritual gifts.

What's in a Name?

We call them "spiritual gifts," but what does the Bible call them? There are four Greek words commonly used in the New Testament to refer to spiritual gifts. A look at each one individually will reveal the full meaning of this concept.

1. *Charisma*

The most familiar term used by Paul is the Greek word *charisma*. Its plural form, *charismata*, is the word from which we derive *charismatic*. *Charisma* refers to a gracious work of God or something God's grace has bestowed. For example, "eternal life" is a *charisma* (Rom. 6:23), as is "deliverance from physical death" (2 Cor. 1:10). Even "celibacy" (1 Cor. 7:7) is a *charisma* (see also Rom. 5:15-16; 11:29; but note especially 1 Cor. 12:4, 9, 28, 30-31).

2. *Pneumatikōn*

In 1 Corinthians 12:1 Paul used the word *pneumatikōn* ("spirituals," i.e., spiritual things), but he shifted to the use of *charisma* in 12:4 and verses following. This is not because Paul denied that gifts come from the Holy Spirit or have a spiritual quality, but it reflects his emphasis that such capacities are the product of God's gracious enabling.[1] What this means is that all gifts are charismatic, not just tongues, healings, and miracles, but also helping, serving, and giving. Hence, in one sense all Christians are charismatic.

3. *Diakonia*

If *charisma* points us to the origin of spiritual gifts, *diakonia*, often translated "ministries," points to their purpose. All spiritual gifts are designed to serve and help others. In 1 Peter 4:10-11 the verb form is used twice of gifted believers "serving" one another. The point is that spiritual gifts are less privileges than responsibilities. Gifts are not for personal adornment, status, power, or popularity.

4. *Energēma*

Spiritual gifts are also described by the term *energēma* (1 Cor. 12:6), translated "effects" (NASB) or "working" (NIV). It points to Paul's emphasis on gifts as the effect or fruit or product of divine power. All spiritual gifts are energized by the power of the Holy Spirit in and through the believer. Here in 1 Corinthians 12:6 Paul wrote, "There are varieties of effects (*energēmatōn*), but the same God who works (*ho energōn*) all things in all persons." Gifts, then, are the concrete operations of divine energy through individual believers.

Paul's emphasis on the fact that it is one and the same Spirit who is the source of the multiplicity of gifts must be noted. It stands as a strong corrective to any form of elitism. Gifts come "through the Spirit" (v. 8a), "according to the same Spirit" (v. 8b), "by the same Spirit" (v. 9a), "by the one Spirit" (v. 9b). Indeed, it is "one and the same Spirit" (v. 11) who distributes gifts according to his will.

If the Holy Spirit is sovereign in giving gifts, he is also sovereign in *withholding* them. All is dependent on what God desires for that moment in his church. We must be hesitant to "claim" a gift, but rather submit to his sovereign will (compare vv. 9 and 11).

When we put these words together we discover that all spiritual gifts (*charismata*) are acts of service or ministry (*diakonia*), which are produced (*energēma*) through us by the Triune God (*pneuma* [Holy Spirit] in v. 4; *kurios* [Lord Jesus] in v. 5; *theos* [God the Father] in v. 6).

In light of this, we may define a spiritual gift as a God-given, and therefore gracious, capacity to serve the body of Christ. It is a divinely empowered or spiritually energized potential to minister to the body of Christ by communicating the knowledge, power, and love of Jesus.

Myths and Misconceptions

Now let's consider a few of the more common misconceptions that surround the subject of spiritual gifts.

Myth #1: Only ordained pastors or other super-saints have miraculous spiritual gifts. Right? Wrong!

The apostle Paul says that to "each one," male and female, young and old (1 Cor. 12:7a) has been given the manifestation of the Spirit. According to Romans 12:3, 6, if you have grace, you have a gift (see also Eph. 4:7; 1 Pet. 4:10). Peter cited the prophecy of Joel on the day of Pentecost to prove that gifts such as prophecy and tongues would be given to "all mankind," including "your sons and your daughters," "young men," "old men," as well as "bondslaves, both men and women" (Acts 2:17-18). Gifts are *not* the exclusive privilege of elders, deacons, pastors, Sunday-school teachers, or some unique class of alleged super-saints.

Some argue that only apostles performed signs and wonders or exercised so-called miraculous gifts. But the New Testament says otherwise. Aside from the apostles, other average Christians who exercised miraculous gifts include 70 followers of Jesus who cast out demons (Luke 10:9,19-20), at least 109 people among the 120 who were gathered in the Upper Room on the day of Pentecost, as well as Stephen (a deacon, Acts 6–7), Phillip (Acts 8), and Ananias (an average layperson, Acts 9). Church members in Antioch heard God's voice and prophesied (Acts 13:1). Followers of John the Baptist in Ephesus (Acts 19:6) prophesied and spoke in tongues; four young, single women at Caesarea were prophetesses (Acts 21:8-9); unnamed brethren of Galatia performed miracles (Gal. 3:5); believers in Rome (Rom. 12:6-8), Corinth (1 Cor. 12–14), and Thessalonica (1 Thess. 5:19-20) prophesied.

Isn't it interesting that Paul so confidently assumes that churches he had neither established nor visited would be charismatic! The apostle couldn't conceive of a church without spiritual gifts. It obviously wasn't necessary for an apostle to be present either to pray or to lay hands on the people in order for such gifts as prophecy to be operative.

Furthermore, 1 Corinthians 12:7-10, suggests nowhere that only apostles are endowed with these gifts. On the contrary, prophecy, faith, miracles, and other supernatural manifestations are given by the sovereign Spirit to *ordinary* Christians in the church for the daily, routine building up of the body. Not merely apostles and elders and deacons, but also homemakers and carpenters and farmers receive the manifestation of the Spirit—all "for the common good" of the church.

Spiritual gifts are not roles. Roles are those opportunities for ministry common to all and available to anyone. All of us are to be witnesses, but not all have the gift of evangelism. All are to give, but not all have the gift of giving. All pray, but not all have the gift of intercession. All have a responsibility to judge and weigh prophetic words and to differentiate among the "spirits" (1 John 4:1-6; 1 Thess. 5:19-22), but not all have the gift of discerning of spirits. All have faith, but not all have the gift of faith. All can teach (Col. 3:16), but not all have the gift of teaching. All can prophesy (1 Cor. 14:24), but not all are prophets. All may receive wisdom (Eph. 1:17), though all may not exercise the gift of word of wisdom.

Likewise, spiritual gifts are not offices. The term *office* is not strictly a biblical one. However, it would appear that an office in the church is characterized by: (1) an element of permanency, (2) recognition by the church (often with a title), (3) being authorized or hallowed in some way, usually through a public ceremony with the laying on of hands, and (4) remuneration for the individual who fills it. Paul refers to Timothy's gift as being "in him" (1 Tim. 4:14; 2 Tim. 1:6). As Gordon Fee explained, "An office is a position that one is called to *fill;* thus it is external to the office holder. This is a *charisma* that indwells Timothy, which he can be commanded 'not to neglect' and encouraged 'to fan into flame.'"[2]

Myth #2: When you were converted, you got all the gifts you will ever get. Right? Wrong!

Quick—name one verse in Scripture where it says all spiritual gifts are given at the moment of conversion. The fact is, on several occasions (1 Cor. 12:31; 14:1, 12-13, 39) we are told to "seek" or "pursue" gifts that we desire but don't yet have. In fact, it's not only biblical; it's mandatory. To a *Christian* audience Paul wrote: "Pursue love, yet desire earnestly spiritual gifts, but especially that you may prophesy" (1 Cor. 14:1). This is not mere permission or even a suggestion: it is a command. If you are not earnestly desiring spiritual gifts, especially prophecy, you are disobeying an apostolic imperative!

In 1 Corinthians 12:31 Paul again wrote, "Earnestly desire the greater gifts." The verb translated "earnestly (or eagerly) desire" (*zēloute*) is grammatically ambiguous. A few insist it is merely a statement characterizing the behavior of the Corinthians, hence, "*You are eager* for the greater gifts." In other words, they take it to be a statement of fact concerning a state of affairs, not an exhortation to future action. But the same verb form appears in 1 Corinthians 14:1 and 14:39 and is there unambiguously imperative (i.e., a command). It is difficult to believe that the same verb, in the same form, in the same context would be used by Paul in two entirely different ways without some hint or contextual clue to that effect.

If you have lingering doubts, carefully read 1 Corinthians 14:13 where Paul commanded the person who speaks in tongues to "pray that he may interpret." This was quite obviously a Christian, for he already had the gift of tongues. But it is equally obvious that he did not have the gift of interpretation, for Paul commanded him to "pray" for it. Clearly, then, at least this one spiritual gift can be given subsequent to conversion. And if one, why not all?

Some have pointed out that the exhortation to "earnestly desire" spiritual gifts (1 Cor. 12:31; 14:1) is in the plural, and thus directed not to individual believers but to the corporate church. They argue that this is grounds for rejecting the idea that Christians should seek any spiritual gift.

But of course the verb is plural, as are virtually all Paul's commands in letters other than those addressed to individuals (such as Philemon, Titus, and Timothy). Paul was writing to *everyone* in the church at Corinth, each of whom was responsible for individually responding to an exhortation that had validity for the entire church. In other words, what is the corporate church if not a collection of *individuals* on *each* of whom the obligation falls? The plural of this exhortation simply indicates that *all* believers in Corinth are to heed the apostolic admonition. It is a duty *common* to everyone. That includes us as well.

Myth #3: Miraculous gifts were given primarily to authenticate apostles. Right? Wrong!

The primary, but not exclusive, purpose of spiritual gifts is to edify others. Gifts are "other-oriented." Some have erroneously concluded from 1 Corinthians 12:7 that it is sinful and selfish ever to enjoy one's gift or to be personally edified from its use. But this is to confuse the *immediate*, or direct, purpose of gifts with their *secondary*, or indirect, effect. It's virtually impossible to faithfully exercise one's spiritual gift, regardless of the context, and not experience a blessing of some sort. If the use of your gift sensitizes your heart to the grace of God and facilitates your maturity in Christ, you can't help but be better equipped to serve and edify others. Although the ultimate purpose of spiritual gifts is to edify others, that is not their only purpose. Jude 20 actually *commands* us to "edify" ourselves!

One primary purpose of miraculous phenomena is to edify and build up the body of Christ. The miraculous gifts of

1 Corinthians 12:7-10 are distributed to average Christians "for the common good" (v. 7), that is, for the welfare and growth of everyone in the church.

Paul explicitly asserted in 1 Corinthians 14:3 that prophecy, one of the miraculous gifts listed in 12:7-10, serves to edify, exhort, and console others in the church. The one who prophesies "edifies the church" (1 Cor. 14:4). We find a similar emphasis in 1 Corinthians 14:5 where Paul said that tongues, when interpreted, also edify the church. In 1 Corinthians 14:26 Paul exhorted those in an assembly to be prepared to minister with a psalm, a teaching, a revelation, a tongue, an interpretation—all of which are designed, he said, for "edification."

Some have questioned whether the gift of tongues was intended to edify believers. If not, why did God provide the gift of interpretation so that tongues might be utilized in the gathered assembly of the church? If the gift was never intended to edify believers, why did Paul himself pray in tongues in the privacy of his own devotions? That he did so is obvious from 1 Corinthians 14:18-19, a passage I'll explain in chapter eight.

My point is this: *all* the gifts of the Spirit, whether tongues or teaching, whether prophecy or mercy, whether healing or helps, were given, among other reasons, for the edification and building up and encouraging and instructing and consoling and sanctifying of the body of Christ. Even if miraculous gifts were no longer needed to attest and authenticate, a point I concede only for the sake of argument, such gifts would continue to function in the church for the other reasons cited.

Myth #4: Seeking spiritual gifts means you probably don't believe in the sovereignty of God. Right? Wrong!

But didn't Paul say that the Holy Spirit decides who will get what gift (see 1 Cor. 12:11, 18)? Yes. But if it is God who bestows gifts according to *his* will, how can we pray for and seek after gifts according to *our* will? The answer is that our desire is itself often the fruit of God's antecedent work in our hearts, stirring us to ask him for what he wants to give. Let's not forget that although salvation is subject to God's sovereign will, we still pray for, preach to, and persuade unbelievers. In fact, as Jack Deere has reminded us, God "does *everything* just as he wills" (see Eph. 1:11),[3] but that doesn't eliminate or diminish our human responsibility to obey the many commands of Scripture.

While we're on this point, it would be good to consider the ways in which the Spirit may choose to impart his gifts to us. On the one hand, Paul simply referred to the Spirit sovereignly "distributing" (1 Cor. 12:11) gifts to people, without saying how. That leaves the door open to any number of possibilities. Perhaps the principal way is in response to our prayers (1 Cor. 14:13). In Romans 1:11 Paul declared his intent to bestow a *charisma* on the Romans upon his arrival in their city. Whereas this may be a reference to some gracious blessing in general, it could as easily be that Paul planned on praying for divine impartation of some specific spiritual gift the Roman church may have needed.

Timothy's gift came to him "through" a prophetic utterance ("through prophecy"), accompanied by the laying on of hands (literally, "with" the laying on of hands, 1 Tim. 4:14). In 1 Timothy 1:18 Paul encouraged Timothy by reminding him of the "prophecies previously made" concerning him. And in 2 Timothy 1:6 Paul referred to a spiritual gift that came to be "in" Timothy "through" the laying on of his hands.

Putting these three texts together, the following scenario unfolds. Evidently, several people prophesied that Timothy was to be the recipient of a particular gift (most likely evangelism, and perhaps leadership). The laying on of hands was probably

an act of confirmation by which the elders and Paul acknowledged this to be true.

Some would see prophecy playing an instrumental role,
through the medium of which this gift was conferred to
Timothy. I've witnessed instances when God simply uses the
occasion of a prophetic utterance to impart a gift. In any case,
we should never hesitate to lay hands on one another and pray
for charismatic impartation.

Myth #5: If people abuse spiritual gifts, they should cease to use spiritual gifts. Right? Wrong!

I find it nothing short of remarkable that to a church obsessed
and glutted with spiritual gifts, to a church awash in spiritual
gifts (1 Cor. 1:5-7), indeed to a church that had *abused* spiritual
gifts, Paul wrote: "Earnestly desire spiritual gifts" (1 Cor. 14:1)!
This is stunning, if only because it is so different from the sort
of counsel we might have given the Corinthians.

The Corinthian believers came in second to no one in the
charismatic race. Yet they had seriously misunderstood and
abused these gifts. My first response is to assume that Paul
would tell them to slow down, if not declare a temporary mora-
torium, on the exercise of these gifts. At the very least he should
have told them to stop praying for and seeking after such miraculous phenomena as tongues and prophecy. So much for my
wisdom!

What he told them to do is really quite amazing. To a church
aflame with charismata, Paul commanded the people to earnestly
seek for more (1 Cor. 12:31; 14:1, 39)! Whereas we might have
doused their zeal with water, Paul appears to pour gasoline on
the fire. The point is this: The solution to the abuse of spiritual
gifts is not prohibition, but correction. Paul simply told them,
"Do it right!" In other words, "Don't do it less. Just do it better!"

I could understand if Paul issued such counsel to a church with great character and little power. But Corinth was a church with little character and great power. This counsel strikes some as unwise, if not dangerous, like throwing a life jacket filled with lead to a drowning man, or saying to a recovering alcoholic, "Hey, buddy, let's go get a drink!" Yet, to the very people guilty of elitism and fanaticism, Paul said, "Be eager and zealous for more gifts than you've already got." We, on the other hand, would most likely have said: "Cool it, Corinthians! Settle down. Forget about gifts. Your spiritual focus is way out of balance. Don't you realize that spiritual gifts are what got you in trouble in the first place!" But, of course, the problem was *not* spiritual gifts. The problem was immature and unspiritual people. The point is that suppression of spiritual zeal is never the answer. *The solution to abuse is not disuse but proper use.*

Recently, a man who had been raised in a charismatic church wrote to me of his decision to leave it. He had become disillusioned with what he believed were counterfeit gifts and people feigning spiritual manifestations. I'm saddened when I hear stories like this. As hard as it may be for us, we must remember that the existence of a fake is not proof of the nonexistence of the real. I'm amazed at how many Christians subconsciously formulate their theological beliefs based not on the beauty of what the Bible describes but in reaction to the ugliness of what they have seen in others who have fabricated an experience or abused some good gift of God.

Be careful that you do not develop unreasonable expectations of anyone who has any particular gift. After all, no matter how spectacular the gift, no matter how marvelous the manifestation of the Spirit, we are but "earthen vessels" (2 Cor. 4:7).

Myth #6: If you have ever used a spiritual gift, you can always use it. Right? Wrong!

Many mistakenly believe that if you have prophesied once, you can prophesy at will, or if you have ever prayed and someone is healed, you can heal at will. The issue at stake here is whether spiritual gifts are *permanent* (what some have called "residential") or *occasional* and *circumstantial*. Can we legitimately say a person *has* a gift, or does one simply *use* a gift? For example, is it possible that someone may on occasion perform a miracle without *having* the gift of miracles?

There are several factors that support the notion of permanency, not least of which are the texts that speak of one "having" a spiritual gift (1 Cor. 13:2; Rom. 12:6). In 1 Corinthians 14:28 Paul seemed to envision the possibility of knowing whether or not one with the gift of interpretation is present in the meeting. Paul exhorted Timothy not to neglect "the spiritual gift *within you*" (1 Tim. 4:14). Paul also said some people have titles that describe a continuing function, such as "teachers," "evangelists," or "prophets" (Eph. 4:11). And in 2 Timothy 1:6-7 Paul clearly affirmed that, notwithstanding neglect and disuse, one's gift (at least Timothy's) can remain. We can't appeal to Romans 11:29 to answer this question, for there the "gifts" of God refer to covenantal blessings bestowed on national Israel.

On the other hand, Paul consistently used the present tense in his discussion of the gifts (1 Cor. 12:11), as if to suggest that gifts are bestowed to meet the need of the moment. Prophecy, for example, is dependent on the spontaneity of revelation (1 Cor. 14:30) and evidently cannot be exercised at will. Healing, too, is always subject to the sovereign will of God. We'll see this more clearly later on.

Perhaps the best answer is to say that some gifts, such as

teaching, leadership, tongues, mercy, and so on are more likely permanent and can be exercised at will, whereas others such as prophecy, healing, and miracles are always subject to the sovereign purpose and timing of the Spirit.

Myth #7: Spiritual gifts aren't necessary now that we have the Bible. Right? Wrong!

I've heard people say, "Miraculous gifts accompanied and attested to the truth of the gospel until the last word of canonical Scripture was written. Now there's no longer a need for such manifestations of divine power. The Bible itself has replaced miraculous phenomena in the life of the church." My immediate problem with this is that the Bible itself makes no such claim!

I'm not denying the role of miraculous gifts in bearing witness to the truth of the gospel in the first century. But why should we think the church in our century stands in any less need of this activity of the Holy Spirit?

Here's something to think about: If miracles were essential in the physical presence of the Son of God, how much more so now in his absence! Are you prepared to suggest that the Bible is capable of doing now in our century what Jesus couldn't do in his? Jesus himself believed it essential to draw upon the miraculous power of the Holy Spirit throughout the course of his earthly ministry. If the glorious presence of the Son of God himself did not preclude the need for miraculous phenomena, how dare we suggest that our possession of the Bible does!

Myth #8: Spiritual gifts always operate at consistent levels of intensity and accuracy. Right? Wrong!

Spiritual gifts often vary in intensity, strength, and accuracy (see 1 Cor. 14:18; 2 Tim. 1:6). This may be what Paul had in mind in Romans 12:6 where he said prophecy should be "according to the proportion of his faith." Paul seems to be saying those with the gift of prophecy had varying levels of trust or confidence that it was truly the Holy Spirit who was working in them to impart a revelation that would become the basis of a prophecy. In other words, there will always be greater and lesser degrees of prophetic ability and consequently greater and lesser degrees of prophetic accuracy. It also seems reasonable to assume that prophetic accuracy may increase or decrease, depending on the circumstances of the person's life, over time. Prophets are to speak in proportion to the confidence and assurance they have that what is said is truly of God. They are not to speak beyond what God has revealed. They must be careful never to speak on their own authority or from their own resources.

It seems obvious that some teachers are more eloquent and effective than others, that some evangelists see a greater harvest of souls, that some church leaders are more successful at mobilizing people for ministry, and the list could go on. One should expect that some will pray more fervently in tongues than others do (as apparently Paul did; see 1 Cor. 14:18), and that some will have a comparatively greater capacity for faith. The efficacy and accuracy of spiritual gifts will vary depending on our personalities, our spiritual maturity, our facility in the Word of God, the depth of intimacy we have with Jesus, and any number of other factors.

What Paul wrote in 2 Timothy 1:6 clearly indicates that one's gift does not always operate at the same level of intensity. Timothy is exhorted to "kindle afresh" his spiritual gift. This would imply that a gift can fluctuate on a sliding scale of relative effectiveness, the latter being in some measure dependent on us. Although a gift is from God, it can be improved upon. We can always learn to use it better and with greater fruit.

Spiritual gifts do not operate automatically or independently of our will and effort. Paul's exhortation to Timothy not to "neglect" his gift (1 Tim. 4:14) suggests that it might become inoperative if he did not diligently utilize it.

Why had Timothy allowed his gift to diminish? Perhaps he had been intimidated. Paul reminded him in verse 7 that he had not been given a spirit of "timidity." Perhaps Timothy had grown fearful that the exercise of the gift (teaching? administration?) would provoke opposition from some in the congregation. Perhaps he had been told he was weak, too young, or incompetent. He may have been led to believe that it would be presumptuous of him to use his gift. Perhaps he had been told his gift was unreal—he only *thought* he had it. In any case, he neglected it. He didn't use it. It was dormant. But it was still "in him."

Some have argued that the "gift" is the Holy Spirit, not a spiritual gift per se. They point to the connection with verse 7 where it is argued that the "spirit" which God gave us is the Holy Spirit (see also v. 14, which seems to connect well with v. 6). But opposing this view are several things. First of all, Paul used the word *charisma*, more likely a reference to a gift than to the Giver. Second, to be in a spiritual condition where you must "kindle afresh" the Spirit suggests that you may have "quenched" him. But this would mean that Paul was saying Timothy was in serious sin. How could Timothy have been so guilty of quenching the Holy Spirit and yet have been so highly commended by Paul as he was in both epistles addressed to him? Third, is it likely that Paul would have related Timothy's reception of the Holy Spirit to the "laying on of his hands" (although this does appear to be the case on a few occasions: Acts 8:17-19; 9:12, 17; 19:6)? Even if one concludes that the "gift of God" in verse 6 refers to the Spirit himself, it would be unwarranted to draw too rigid a distinction between the Spirit and the gift that he enables one to exercise. After all, each gift is a manifestation of the Spirit.

Myth #9: Those with more spectacular gifts are more spiritual. Right? Wrong!

This is a myth that few people will affirm but many believe. It's not unusual for those with gifts such as mercy and exhortation and helps to feel inferior to those with prophecy and teaching and tongues. Worse still is that those with the latter gifts often make other people feel that way. People with gifts that draw attention and applause are especially prone to measure personal value by gifting (or lack of it).

This was certainly a problem in ancient Corinth. Their tendency (ours too!) was to elevate their esteem for people whose gifts were characterized by a greater and more conspicuous supernatural display. We mistakenly think that if the manifestation of the Spirit is more explicit, then the individual is more mature, or at least more favored of God, or surely, if nothing else, more useful to the church. Or we think that because someone has more than one gift that person has more of the Holy Spirit. The fact is that a person with ten gifts may be less mature than a person with only one.

Perhaps the most effective response to this myth is the constant reminder of Paul's rebuke of the Corinthians themselves: "For who regards you as superior? And what do you have that you did not receive? But if you did receive it, why do you boast as if you had not received it?" (1 Cor. 4:7). We would all do well to heed Paul's counsel.

Myth #10: The only spiritual gifts God will ever give are those explicitly mentioned in the Bible. Right? Wrong!

Well, maybe that's wrong. On this point I have to be careful. I'm not as convinced this is a myth as I am the others. But why must we conclude that God can only give those gifts that are listed in the New Testament? In Romans 12:6-8 Paul mentioned prophecy, service, teaching, exhortation, giving, leading, and showing mercy. In 1 Corinthians 12:8-10 we read of word of wisdom, word of knowledge, faith, gifts of healings, effecting of miracles, prophecy, distinguishing of spirits, tongues, and interpretation of tongues. In the same chapter Paul again mentioned apostles,[4] prophecy, teaching, miracles, gifts of healings, helps, administration, and tongues (12:28). First Peter 4:10-11 refers to only two: speaking and serving (perhaps general categories rather than specific gifts). Finally, Ephesians 4:11 lists apostle, prophet, evangelist, pastor, teacher (or possibly, pastor-teacher).

The lists contain an amazing mixture of what we might regard as supernatural and natural gifts. That is to say, some gifts appear to be more overt expressions of divine power than others. But the intriguing thing is that Paul made no such distinction. Regardless of what the gift may be, it is the same God who works all things in all men.

But are these lists exhaustive? What about intercession? Is it a spiritual gift to have the capacity to intercede with almost ceaseless energy resulting in a track record of answered prayers? What about other ministries and activities not specifically listed as among the charismata, such as effectiveness in deliverance? I've known people who have a remarkable and extraordinary anointing to help others experience freedom from demonic oppression.

Some might argue that we can't go beyond what the Bible

says. But as long as we do not go *against* what the Bible says, why must we think that God is either incapable or unwilling to impart new gifts not explicitly listed in Scripture? Might there not be new situations, new needs, differing circumstances in differing times and places that call for a wider array of manifestations of the Spirit than those Paul described in his own day? I can't prove it, and that's why I'm hesitant to put this myth in the same category as the others. On the other hand, I see no reason to insist that the lists noted above are *all* the gifts that God will ever give. There's simply no way to know for sure. One thing is certain, however. If there are other gifts God gives, they must conform to the same principles and rules of practice set forth in the Bible by which all gifts are judged.

THREE

Words of Wisdom and Knowledge

It showed no signs of being anything other than a routine day, until a strange car pulled up outside our church. A distraught father escorted into my office his twenty-year-old son who appeared to be struggling with numerous psychological problems that some thought were the result of demonic oppression. This young man was unable to perform the routine tasks of daily life and was desperate for insight into what the source of his problem might be.

As we were praying, the name *Megan* popped into my head. [I've taken the liberty to alter the names of those involved in this story.] The inescapable impression on my heart was that this lady was the cause of his problem and that in some way through his questionable involvement with her, she had exposed him to demonic influence.

A few moments later, he began to tell me his story. He referred to his girlfriend several times (but not by name), and it was obvious she played a crucial role in his life. Finally I asked him what her name was. "Megan," he said. As it turned out, Megan, who was heavily involved in the occult, had seduced him into an immoral relationship. The encounter had taken place in the home of her mother, who also was deeply immersed in occult practices. With this understanding of the significance of Megan, I understood the Lord was directing my prayers, and I was able to pray for him more intelligibly and with greater fruit.

About thirty minutes later, another name sprang into my mind. This time it was *Derek*—coming with no less clarity than had *Megan*. This time, though, I didn't feel as if Derek were a part of the problem, but rather of the solution. Unlike before, I didn't hesitate on this one. "Does the name *Derek* mean anything special to you?" I asked. His eyes widened and his face lit up: "Oh my, yes! He is my dearest friend—a man older than myself who has been praying for me through this entire mess. In fact, we were on our way to his house to get his advice when we stopped off to talk with you."

Both of these words were used by God to help this young man deal with his problems. What should we call it? Some would say it was the word of knowledge (1 Cor. 12:8) or even the word of wisdom, whereas others call such phenomena prophecy. On two occasions Paul simply referred to a "revelation" coming to a believer unrelated to any specific gift (see 1 Cor. 14:6, 26; in 14:30 the "revelation" comes in conjunction with prophecy). Could it be there are what we might call "revelatory" gifts distinct from the three noted above? In any case, how do we classify what I experienced when praying for that young man?

Biblical Precedents

The problem we face in defining and describing these two gifts of the Spirit is simply this: The only place they are mentioned in the New Testament is in 1 Corinthians 12:8, where Paul provided us with neither a definition nor information about how they are to function in the body of Christ. Nothing in the terms *word, wisdom,* and *knowledge* themselves provides us with theological insight into how they are being used in this passage. For this, we must look elsewhere in 1 Corinthians.

The fallout is that most students of the New Testament appeal to scriptural anecdotes they believe are examples of these gifts in operation. The problem is that none of these passages mentions word of wisdom or word of knowledge. Some examples thought to be expressions of these gifts include:

(1) Matthew 9:1-8. Here Jesus is described as "knowing" the "thoughts" of the scribes, in response to which he speaks a powerful rebuke.

(2) Matthew 12:22-37. Again, Jesus, "knowing their thoughts" (v. 25), spoke a word of rebuke and instruction.

(3) Luke 6:6-11. Here it is said that Jesus "knew what they were thinking" (v. 8).

(4) Luke 9:46-48. Again, Jesus is described as "knowing what they [his disciples] were thinking in their heart" (v. 47).

(5) John 1:43-51. This is the story of the calling of Nathanael where Jesus, without having met the man, knew his moral character and described having "seen" him sitting under a fig tree.

(6) John 4. Here is the most frequently cited example—where Jesus told the Samaritan woman the secret sins of her life.

(7) Acts 5:1-11. It would appear that in some way, most likely by revelation, Peter gained knowledge about the secret and sinful activity of Ananias and Sapphira and spoke a word of judgment accordingly.

(8) Acts 8:26-40. The Spirit gave Philip instructions concerning the Ethiopian. Was that an example of a word of knowledge?

(9) Acts 9:10-19. Ananias was given "knowledge" in a vision of a man named Saul and received divine guidance and instruction on what to say.

(10) Acts 10. Were the revelatory experiences of Cornelius and Peter in Acts 10 examples of words of knowledge?

(11) Acts 13:1-3. Was the word that came to the church at Antioch concerning the mission of Paul and Barnabas an example of this gift?

(12) Acts 13:6-12. Paul was given revelatory insight into the heart of Elymas the magician and spoke a word of judgment.

(13) Acts 14:8-10. Some have suggested that Paul's revelatory insight and word to the lame man was a word of knowledge.

(14) Acts 16:16-18. Paul received revelatory insight into the cause of the slave girl's ability and spoke accordingly. Was this a word of knowledge?

Are these merely instances of revelatory activity of a general sort (as noted above), or are they occurrences of the gift of prophecy? Or could they be examples of the word of wisdom or word of knowledge? Yet again, perhaps they are instances of the gift of discerning of spirits. Might they be expressions of miraculous activity that is a combination of some or all of these revelatory events? Each of these instances is undoubtedly revelatory in nature, which is to say that God disclosed information otherwise unattainable. But should we call any of these incidents *word of wisdom* or *word of knowledge*?

Wisdom and Knowledge in Corinth

We can find a little help by returning to first-century Corinth and noting how these words were used among Christians there. It would appear that the people in Corinth were influenced by an incipient Gnosticism that emphasized both wisdom and knowledge as the keys to true spirituality. British New Testament scholar James Dunn refers to these two terms as "slogans of the faction opposing Paul in Corinth."[1] Dunn argues that "this is why *gnōsis* [knowledge] keeps recurring within the Corinthian letters and only rarely elsewhere, and why 1 Corinthians 1–3 is so dominated by discussion of *sophia* [wisdom]."[2] Remarkably, it was actually in the name of wisdom that the Corinthians were rejecting both Paul and his gospel.[3]

The word *wisdom* can be used in both a good and a bad sense. Evil wisdom is the rhetorical skill, eloquence, and natural reasoning used to undermine the gospel. Worldly wisdom is the perspective of the unbelieving mind that knows nothing of the realm of the Spirit and regards the idea of a crucified Messiah as absurd. Spiritual wisdom, on the other hand, refers primarily to the mysterious purposes of God whereby he redeems his people through the foolishness of the cross (see especially 1 Cor. 2:6-9).

Perhaps our interpretation of the gift of "word of wisdom" in 12:8 should reflect Paul's emphasis on the "message" (word) of "wisdom" in 1 Corinthians 1–3. Mark Stibbe agrees and defines the gift of word of wisdom as follows:

> This means that the "word of wisdom" should be defined as *a charismatic revelation into God's secret, redemptive purposes in history.* It should be seen first and foremost as an inspired word concerning the secret heavenly wisdom behind the death of an emaciated carpenter in ancient Palestine.[4]

Or again, word of wisdom may be the ability to articulate life-changing insights into God's mysterious, saving purposes for mankind, both on a global plane as well as in application to individuals.

The same may be noted of the word *knowledge*. In 1 Corinthians 8:1-4, 7, 10 *knowledge* appears four times (see also 13:2, 8). Knowledge, according to Paul, is insight into the unfathomable depths of God's gracious work in Christ. Thus the word of knowledge may be "the special ability to put into words divinely revealed knowledge about God's grace."[5]

If so, it may be that when Paul came to 1 Corinthians 12 he decided to reclaim for distinctly Christian use both the terms *wisdom* and *knowledge* and apply them in a way that would build up the church. Dunn agrees and defines the word of wisdom as "some charismatic utterance giving an insight into, some fresh understanding of, God's plan of salvation or of the benefits it brings to believers."[6] He defines word of knowledge in similar fashion, focusing on the idea of insight into the nature of the world, both spiritual and natural, with special reference to the relationship between God and man. A word of knowledge, says Dunn, was simply an utterance spoken under inspiration that communicated an insight into "cosmical realities and relationships."[7] It might even more closely approximate the idea of inspired teaching, in which the speaker is granted extraordinary insight into the meaning of Scripture.

If these definitions are accurate, and I'm not entirely convinced they are, we may need to refer to those revelatory insights into the details, data, and secrets of a person's life, not as word of knowledge or word of wisdom, but as prophecy or simply as a revelation.

Revelatory Words?

But there is still another question. Are the word of wisdom and word of knowledge *revelatory* gifts? That is to say, does the insight or illumination or knowledge come immediately and spontaneously from the Holy Spirit apart from natural means, or is it the reasoned conclusion to which any Christian, through observation and study of the Scriptures, might come?

Before answering that question, observe that Paul did not call wisdom and knowledge spiritual gifts per se. He spoke of the word (*logos*) of wisdom and the word (*logos*) of knowledge. As Dunn explains: "For Paul wisdom and knowledge as such are not to be thought of as charismata; only the actual utterance which reveals wisdom or knowledge to others is a charisma."[8] Dunn wants to distinguish between that general wisdom and knowledge which all Christians possess (or *may* possess) and the gift of utterance in relation to wisdom and knowledge, which is restricted in scope.

It may well be that word of wisdom and word of knowledge are *not* revelatory in nature.[9] However, we should note that Paul's use of *knowledge* later on in his discussion of spiritual gifts (13:2, 8-12; 14:6) would seem to support the *supernatural, spontaneous,* and *revelatory* nature of this gift. In 1 Corinthians 13:2 Paul mentioned having all knowledge in the same breath with prophecy and faith, both overtly supernatural giftings. Again, in verses 8-12, knowledge is linked with tongues and prophecy to make the point regarding the continuation of the charismata until the second coming of Christ. Although no reference is made to the *word of* knowledge, it seems likely that Paul's use of *knowledge* points back to 12:8. We especially note 14:6 where *knowledge* is sandwiched, so to speak, between *revelation* and *prophecy*. My sense is that this knowledge is the fruit of a revelatory event that 12:8 indicates is to be spoken ("word" or "message" of knowledge) for the edification of the church.

The customary Pentecostal, charismatic, third-wave understanding of the word of wisdom and the word of knowledge is that they refer, respectively, to the articulation of revelatory insight into the *how* (wisdom) and *what* (knowledge) of a person's life. Word of wisdom, so it has been said, pertains to *instruction*, and word of knowledge pertains to *information*. But in view of Paul's use of the terms *word*, *wisdom*, and *knowledge* elsewhere in 1 Corinthians, we may need to be more cautious and less dogmatic in how we define these gifts. In the light of what we've seen, how would *you* classify or describe the following three examples?

A Gifted Baptist

Consider this incident from the ministry of Charles Spurgeon, perhaps the greatest preacher of the nineteenth century (some would say, of *any* century). While preaching at Exeter Hall in London he once broke off his sermon and pointed in a certain direction, declaring: "Young man, those gloves you are wearing have not been paid for: you have stolen them from your employer."

After the service, an obviously pale and agitated young man approached Spurgeon and begged to speak with him privately. He placed a pair of gloves on the table and said, "It's the first time I have robbed my master, and I will never do it again. You won't expose me, sir, will you? It would kill my mother if she heard that I had become a thief." Spurgeon could not have learned this information about the young man from reading the Bible. It was undeniably spontaneous, overtly supernatural, and revelatory.[10]

"Walks With a Cough"

It's not unusual for a gift of healing to be imparted in conjunction with the operation of a revelatory gift, whether the latter be word of knowledge or prophecy. A young lady who was attending one of our church conferences in 1997 was frustrated that her asthmatic condition was so severe that she was unable to sing in worship without the use of an inhaler. On Friday she cried out to God for healing from her affliction but did not describe her condition to anyone at the conference.

She had suffered from asthma since the age of twelve, but when she reached seventeen the condition had noticeably worsened. It was then that she began to experience chronic bronchitis (suffering from it eight to nine months each year) and repeated bouts of pneumonia. She coughed almost constantly, eventually requiring the use of steroids and antibiotics on a monthly basis. It was so bad that she couldn't climb a flight of stairs without using the inhaler. Taking his cue from the movie, *Dances With Wolves,* her husband affectionately nicknamed her "Walks With a Cough."

She gave birth to a son and soon discovered that he suffered from asthma as well. At the age of two his left lung collapsed. Soon he was being treated with heavy doses of steroids and four breathing treatments a day, as well as multiple antibiotics.

At the close of the conference, on Sunday morning, two days after her prayer of desperation, a man came to the microphone and spoke this word:

There is a lady here today whose name I don't know, but the Lord has told me she has dark hair [which she does]. He also indicated that when you were seventeen years old you became quite ill, which aggravated your chronic respiratory problems. I would like to pray for you. It may be that the Lord will heal you today.

After hesitating momentarily, she went forward and identified herself to the man. She also requested prayer for her then four-year-old son. She was instantly healed as the man and his wife prayed for her. In the five years since that day she has had no recurrence of asthma or pneumonia. Her son has needed neither steroids nor the breathing treatments that once were a routine part of his daily life.

An Amazing Life

My friend Nancy has endured incredible suffering in her life and yet remains strong in the Lord. But even those who are strong need encouragement now and then. At a conference in 1998, I was sitting with Nancy when she was given a "word" by Paul Cain, a remarkably gifted evangelist.[11] Although he had never met Nancy, he asked her to stand up: "Nancy, I saw the March winds blowing. March is a special month for you. The Lord is going to bless you and give you the spirit of Nathan."

This is an excellent example of how a revelation might come accurately to someone who is, however, uncertain of its interpretation. When Paul heard the Spirit speak the name *Nathan* he thought it had something to do with the Old Testament prophet who confronted David. What he didn't know, until we informed him later that day, is that *Nathan* was the name of Nancy's son who had been killed in a tragic car accident.

The next day Paul again called out Nancy and asked her to stand. "I saw that precious young man that was taken from you," said Paul. "The Lord said, 'I gave him to her in the springtime of the year. And I took him in the middle of the year.'" Paul continued: "I got a glimpse of him [Nathan] standing before the Lord, and he looks like he's thirty-three years old. That's all he's ever going to look from now on. That's not a doctrine," Paul was careful to add, "but that's how old he looks at this time."

Here's the significance of what Paul said. March is indeed quite special to Nancy. Her birthday is March 10, and her husband passed away on March 4, 1983. The Lord revealed to Paul that Nathan had been "given" to Nancy in the "spring" of the year. Nathan's birthday is April 21! "I took him in the middle of the year," said the Lord. Nathan died on June 4, 1983, only three months after Nancy's husband had died.

As would be true of any mother devastated by the loss of a child, Nancy often had wondered if Nathan truly knew Jesus before his death. Paul's word of encouragement is that he did. As a way of confirming it, the Lord had shown Paul that on this day in 1998 Nathan looked "thirty-three years old." Do your math. If Nathan were eighteen in 1983, had he lived he would have been exactly thirty-three when Paul spoke this word!

I know there are skeptics who will immediately question this incident. "How do we know Paul Cain didn't investigate this woman's past and find out information that he later passed off as revelation?" Perhaps it would be asking too much of you if I were to say you can trust me on this one. All I know is that I have seen Paul do this on several hundred occasions (yes, several *hundred*) and can personally vouch for his integrity. But for those who simply cannot (or will not) believe that God still speaks today, no one's testimony will suffice.

For the rest of you, the question still remains: How do we categorize these experiences? We look at each one and ask, Was it a word of wisdom, word of knowledge, or a prophecy? It may be that we will never know. It may be that we don't *need* to know. What's important for us to know, however, is that God still speaks, and does so for the benefit and blessing and encouragement of his children. Let our prayer be, "Oh, Lord, speak! For thy servant heareth!"

FOUR

Faith and Healing

There is no such thing as the gift of healing. There never has been. Don't panic! Give me a chance to explain what I mean. You won't be disappointed.

Prophetic Providence

My expectations concerning divine healing were radically impacted by what I call an act of *prophetic providence*. I was still pastoring in Ardmore, Oklahoma, still somewhat skeptical about the reality of healing for today. It was Friday, October 26, 1990, and I was busily preparing my Sunday sermon. I was preaching through Acts and had reached the story of the paralytic in chapter three. Here was a forty-year-old man, paralyzed from the womb, who was healed through the ministry of Peter and John. My sermon preparation wasn't going very well. I was literally in midsentence, writing the words I would soon speak to my congregation, words that denied—or at least cast a long shadow of doubt—on the possibility that God might heal someone like that today. Then came a knock at the door.

My secretary entered with the day's mail. I was a little surprised, because the mail didn't normally arrive until well after 1:00 P.M. Here it was just after 11:00 A.M. For some reason I put my pen down and opened the one and only letter that arrived that day. It was from an elderly lady in Wales, of all places. I certainly didn't know anyone in Wales. I'd never been to Wales. But someone had sent this lady a copy of the book I had written *against* healing. I'm not proud of that book. (Thankfully, it's out of print.)

The letter was short and to the point. She kindly affirmed some of what she read in my book but went on to humbly suggest that she believed God would respond with power to our prayers for healing. After reading the letter, I noticed something else in the envelope. It was the written testimony of a lady named Margery Steven. In 1955, she was afflicted with an extraordinarily severe case of multiple sclerosis. She had to be lifted in and out of a wheelchair, her legs having become utterly useless. Straps were used to keep her from falling out of the chair. Her left arm was completely useless, her left eye was closed, and vision in her right eye was virtually gone. She would often lose consciousness for hours at a time.

Five years into her illness, on February 4, 1960, Margery had a powerful dream during the night. She saw herself sitting in a chair beside her bed, completely healed. When she awakened, she heard a voice filling the room, a voice she believed to be that of Jesus. He said: "Tarry a little longer." But she seemed only to get worse from that day on. Eventually her speech became so impaired that it was virtually impossible to understand a word she said. Perhaps it would be better if I let you read in her own words what happened next.

On Monday, July 4, exactly five months after God had spoken to me, my Lord healed me, in the very chair of which I had dreamed! I had said goodbye to my husband at five minutes to six on that Monday morning—a helpless woman. At 6:15 my mother gave me a cup of tea. At 6:20 my father and mother lifted me from my bed, strapped me in the chair beside the bed, put a bell in my good hand, to summon aid if needed, and left me alone. Mother went to get my washing water and my father had gone to get a towel from upstairs. *Then in a matter of seconds, when I was all on my own, my Lord Jesus healed me!* I felt a warm glow go over my body. My left foot, which was doubled up, straightened out; my right foot, the toes of which were pointed towards my heel, came back into position. I grasped the handle of my bedroom door which was beside me, undid the straps which were about my body, and said, "By faith I will stand," which I did.

With that I thought of my mother and the shock it would be to her if she came back to find her daughter standing after so many years, so I sat down and called for her. With that, both my parents came running to my room, thinking I was in need of them. I said, "Mum, dear, take my hands. Please don't be afraid; something wonderful has happened." I put out my right arm and as I did so my left arm came out from behind me and joined the other! It was so wonderful a few minutes afterwards to find I could wear my own wedding ring, which I had not been able to do for years, as my fingers of that hand had got so thin.

My mother said, "Darling, how wonderful, your hand is warm, and is well again." I said, "Mum, dear, it's more wonderful than that. *I can stand.*" With that, holding her hands, *I stood once more on my two feet.* Then, gently putting my parents to one side, I said, "Dears, I do not need your help anymore. I'm walking with God." Unaided I then walked from my bedroom, through the small dining room to the kitchen, my parents following mutely behind me. When I reached the kitchen I turned and went back into the dining room and taking off my glasses I said,

"Mum, I can trust God for my hands and feet. I can trust Him for my sight." *With that, in a moment, my left eye opened and my sight was fully restored!* In fact Jesus made such a perfect job I do not need the glasses I had before I was ill and I am now writing dozens of letters a day! To Him be all the glory!

The Welsh lady who sent me this testimony informed me in her letter that Margery Steven was still alive and well, thirty years after her healing.

I sat at my desk more than a little stunned. It couldn't have been mere coincidence. In the marvelous providence of God, someone had sent my book to this lady at *just the right time* so that she would send to me *at just the right time* a copy of this testimony. *I just so happened* (!) to be writing the very words that would undermine people's faith in God's willingness to heal today when the letter arrived, not from someone in my own church who knew what I was preaching or even from someone in the United States, but from someone I'd never met in Wales!

I try not to read into events more than I should, but no one will ever convince me this was anything less than the providential timing of a God who was determined to put some sense into a preacher's head and some passion into his heart. It worked.

The Gift of Faith

Before I say anything more about healing, a few words about the gift of faith are in order. Although the New Testament has much to say about faith in general, it doesn't explicitly refer to the charisma, or gift, of faith outside this passage in 1 Corinthians 12.

Therefore, the best way to identify and define the nature of this gift is to look briefly at how faith is portrayed elsewhere. Generally speaking, the New Testament mentions three kinds of faith, or, better still, three distinct contexts or circumstances in which faith is exercised. I will use Mark Stibbe's[1] terminology and distinguish between conversion faith, continuing faith, and charismatic faith.

Conversion faith is the faith through which we are justified. This is the faith identified in Scripture as that trust or confidence or belief in the atoning sacrifice of Christ that occurs at the moment of conversion. This is the faith Paul referred to in Ephesians 2:8-9: "By grace you have been saved through faith, and that not of yourselves; it is the gift of God, not as a result of works, that no one should boast" (see also Rom. 1:16-17; 3:28; 5:1; etc.). Unlike the *charisma* of faith, which is restricted to those believers to whom the Spirit wills to give it (1 Cor. 12:11), every Christian has this kind of faith.

Continuing faith is the faith we exercise daily as we look confidently to God to do in and through our lives all that he has promised to do. This is the faith that is one of the fruits of the Spirit (Gal. 5:22). This is the faith of Hebrews 11 (compare with 1 Pt. 1:8 and others). All believers have this faith, but in varying degrees of intensity. Some are more and others less confident in the goodness and greatness of God throughout the course of daily life.

Charismatic faith is the faith, noted in several texts, that appears to be spontaneous and functions as the divinely enabled condition on which the more overtly supernatural activities of God are suspended. This, I believe, is the "gift of faith" in 1 Corinthians 12:9. Consider these possible examples of the gift of faith:

And Jesus answered saying to them, "Have faith in God. Truly I say to you, whoever says to this mountain, 'Be taken up and cast into the sea,' and does not doubt in his heart, but believes that what he says is going to happen, it shall be granted him. Therefore I say to you, all things for which you pray and ask, believe that you have received them, and they shall be granted you" (Mark 11:22-24; also Matt. 17:20-21; 21:21-22).

And if I have the gift of prophecy, and know all mysteries and all knowledge; and if I have all faith, so as to remove mountains, but do not have love, I am nothing (1 Cor. 13:2).

And the prayer offered in faith will restore the one who is sick, and the Lord will raise him up, and if he has committed sins, they will be forgiven him (James 5:15).

Charismatic faith, or the gift of faith, like the other charismata, is not given to every member of the body of Christ. However, it would appear that any member of the body of Christ is a potential candidate for the experience of this manifestation of the Spirit. The gift of faith should probably be regarded, more so than most other gifts of the Spirit, as occasional or spontaneous, rather than permanent or residential.

This is a special faith that "enables a believer to trust God to bring about certain things for which he or she cannot claim some divine promise recorded in Scripture, or some state of affairs grounded in the very structure of the gospel."[2] In other words, it is the "God-given ability, without fakery or platitudinous exhortations, to believe what you do not really believe, to trust God for a certain blessing *not* promised in Scripture."[3]

The gift of faith is that *mysterious surge of confidence* that rises within a person in a particular situation of need or challenge and which gives an *extraordinary certainty and assurance* that God is about to act through a word or an action.

Linking Faith and Healing

I believe there is a close connection between gifts of healings (as well as the gift of miracles) and the gift of faith, which immediately precedes them in Paul's list of the charismata.

The role of faith in healing is crucial, and it is manifest in a number of ways. On occasion the faith of the person needing healing is instrumental (Matt. 9:22); while at other times it is the faith of a friend or family member (Matt. 15:28; Mark 2:5, 11). Sometimes the focus is on the faith of the person praying for the one who needs healing (Mark 9:17-24), and on certain occasions, faith apparently plays no part at all in the healing (John 5:1-9; indeed, in the Gospel of John, faith is *never* mentioned as a condition for healing; see also Matt. 8:14). The point is that on some occasions, God simply heals by a sovereign act of his will unrelated to anything in us. However, in the vast majority of cases, Jesus healed people because of *someone's* faith.

In the case of both Jairus and the woman suffering from bleeding (Mark 5), faith was directed toward Jesus as an expression of need. Again, in Luke 17:11-19 Jesus healed ten lepers. When one returned to say thanks, Jesus said: "Your faith has made you well" (v. 19). When Bartimaeus asked Jesus to heal him of his blindness, Jesus said: "Go, your faith has healed you" (Mark 10:52, NIV). In the famous story of the paralytic being lowered through the roof, Jesus healed him when he saw that the man's friends had faith (Mark 2:5).

Five Kinds of Faith for Healing

I believe that faith for healing operates at any one of five levels. There is, first of all, faith that God is your sole source for blessing, that he is your hope and he alone (see Ps. 33:18-22; 147:10-11). Why did Jesus emphasize faith? Neither he nor his Father need it. They could have orchestrated life such that something other than faith would be the condition on which they would heal. They are not hampered or hindered by the faithlessness or prayerlessness of the sick person or those who pray for his or her healing. The reason is this: faith glorifies God. Faith points us away from ourselves to him. Faith turns us away from our own power and resources to his. Faith says, "Lord, I am nothing and you are everything. I entrust myself to your care. I cling to you alone. My confidence is in your word and character no matter what happens."

Faith is not a weapon by which we demand things from God or put him in subjection to us. Faith is an act of self-denial. Faith is a renunciation of one's ability to do anything and a confession that God can do everything. Faith derives its power *not from the spiritual energy of the person who believes but from the supernatural efficacy of the object of belief—God!* It is not faith's act but its object that accounts for the miraculous.

Second, there is *faith in God's ability to heal.* Jesus took special delight in healing those who trusted in his *power,* people who were open and receptive to his power to perform a mighty work. In Matthew 9:28-29 Jesus asked the two blind men only if they believed he was *able* to heal them. He wanted to find out what they thought about him, whether or not they trusted his *ability.* "Yes, Lord," came their response. Jesus replied, "Be it done to you according to your faith," and they were instantly healed. Jesus regarded their confidence in his power to help them as "faith" and dealt mercifully with them on that basis.

"Jesus, I believe you are able to heal me" is the kind of faith that pleases him. I can almost hear Jesus say, "Yes! I was waiting to hear you say that. It's important to me that you truly believe that I am capable of doing this." The leper in Matthew 8 said to Jesus, "Lord, *if You are willing, you can make me clean*" (v. 2). The leper didn't question Christ's ability. He trusted that completely. He did have doubts about the willingness of Jesus to do it. But Jesus didn't rebuke him for such doubts, as if it were a shortcoming in his faith that might jeopardize his healing. He healed him because of the leper's confidence that he *could* do it.

As we already noted, the hemorrhaging woman was healed when she simply touched Jesus' garment. "Your faith has healed you" (Mark 5:34, NIV), said Jesus. In other words, "What I enjoy and respond to is your simple confidence and trust in my ability to make a difference in your life."

Third, there is *faith in God's heart for healing*. This is *faith in God's goodness and his desire to bless his children* (see Ps. 103; Luke 11:11-13). This is faith or belief or confidence that it is God's character to build up, not tear down; to bring unity, not division; to create wholeness and completeness, not disintegration and disarray. Every time Jesus healed we catch a glimpse into his heart. Healing is a window into the soul of our Savior: it reveals the depth of his care and compassion for people. People came to Jesus for healing because they knew they would find in him someone who would understand their pain, their frustration, their grief, their confusion. Their healing flowed out of their personal encounter with a caring, loving, person. Jesus embodied for them concern, compassion, and power.

Fourth, there is *the faith not simply that God can heal, not simply that God delights to heal, but faith that God does heal*. This is the *faith that healing is part of God's purpose and plan for his people today.* You can believe God is able to heal and that he delights to heal and still not believe that healing is for the church today. For example, I believe that God is able to make manna fall from heaven to feed his people. I believe that God delights in providing food for his people; he doesn't want them to go hungry or to starve. But I do not have faith that God does, in fact, intend to send manna from heaven as a means of providing our physical needs. Therefore, I will not spend time praying that he do so.

Fifth and finally, there is *the faith that it is his will to heal right now.* I have in mind the psychological certainty that healing is what God is, in fact, going to do now. This is probably more of what Paul had in mind when he spoke of the gift of faith in 1 Corinthians 12:9. It may also be what James referred to as "the prayer offered in faith" (James 5:15).

The prayer of faith isn't one that we pray whenever *we* want to. It is a unique prayer, divinely energized only on those occasions when it is God's sovereign purpose to impart a gift for healing. James was careful to place the definite article (translated *the*) before both *prayer* and *faith* (hence, *"the* prayer of *the* faith"). One prays *this* prayer only when prompted by the Spirit-wrought conviction that God *intends* to heal the one for whom prayer is being offered. This is more than merely believing that God is able to heal; this appears to be faith that he, in this particular case, is not only willing to heal, but willing to heal *right now.* God sovereignly bestows this faith necessary for healing *only when he wills.* When God chooses to heal, he produces in the heart(s) of those praying the faith or confidence that healing is precisely his intent. The particular kind of faith to which James refers, in response to which God heals, is not the kind that we may exercise at our will. It is the kind of faith that we exercise only when God wills.

One Sunday a couple came to me before the service and asked that the elders of our church anoint their infant son and pray for his healing. After the service we gathered in the back room and I anointed him with oil. I don't recall the precise medical name for his condition, but at six months of age he had a serious liver disorder that could require immediate surgery if something didn't change. As we prayed, something very unusual happened. As we laid hands on this young child, I found myself suddenly filled with an overwhelming and inescapable confidence that he would be healed. It was totally unexpected. Not wanting to be presumptuous, I tried to doubt but couldn't. I prayed confidently, filled with a faith unshakeable and undeniable. I said silently to God, "Lord, you really are going to heal him." Although the family left the room unsure, I was absolutely *certain* God had healed him. The next morning the doctor agreed. He was totally healed and is a healthy, happy young boy today.

If this were an example of the gift of faith working in conjunction with a gift of healing, there is no reason to think that had I prayed for another afflicted infant boy that day he would necessarily have been healed. The fact that I received a gift for healing on this one occasion did not guarantee that I could pray with equal success on some other occasion.

Let me make three additional comments about this passage in James 5. First, James made several key points about the relationship of sickness to sin in verse 15. He wrote, "The prayer offered in faith will restore the one who is sick, and the Lord will raise him up, and *if* he [the sick man] has committed sins, they will be forgiven him" (v. 15, emphasis added). James is in harmony with Jesus (John 9:1-3) and Paul (2 Cor. 12:1-10) that not all sickness is the direct result of sin. Sometimes it is (1 Cor. 11:27-30; Mark 2:1-12) but not always. The "if" in verse 15 is not designed to suggest the one who is sick may *never* have sinned. The meaning is that if God should heal him in answer to prayer, this indicates that any sins of the sufferer, which might have been responsible for this particular illness, were forgiven. In other words, if sin were responsible for his sickness, the fact that God healed him physically would be evidence that God had forgiven him spiritually.

Second, the sin James had in mind may be that of bitterness, resentment, jealousy, anger, or unforgiveness in our relationships with one another, or conceivably any number of sins we may have committed against God. Hence, James advised us to "confess [our] sins to one another" (James 5:16). He probably had in mind either confessing to the person against whom you have sinned or confessing to another believer your more general transgressions, or violations, of biblical laws. What this tells us is that God has chosen to suspend healing mercy on the repentance of his people. When the hurting don't get healed, it may be a result of stubbornness and spiritual insensitivity more than because "God doesn't do that sort of thing anymore."

Finally, we should take careful note of the example of Elijah (see James 5:17-18). The argument has been made by cessationists that biblical miracles were clustered, or concentrated, in only three major periods of history: the days of Moses and Joshua, the time of Elijah and Elisha, and the time of Christ and the apostles. The point of this argument is that Elijah and Elisha, for example, were special, extraordinary, unique individuals who cannot serve as models for us when we pray.[4]

But James said precisely the opposite! The point of verses 17-18 is to counter the argument that Elijah was somehow unique or that because of the period in which he lived he could pray with miraculous success but we cannot. James wanted readers to know that Elijah was just like you and me. He was a human being with weaknesses, fears, doubts, failures—no less than we. In other words, James said: "Don't let anyone tell you Elijah was in a class by himself. He wasn't. He's just like you. You are just like him. Therefore, pray like he did!"

Don't forget the context: James appealed to the example of Elijah to encourage us when we pray for the sick! The point is that we should pray for miraculous healing with the same faith and expectation with which Elijah prayed for the end of a three-year drought.

The (?) Gift of Healing

This brings us back to my earlier assertion that there is no such thing as the gift of healing. I said this both because of the way Paul described this spiritual phenomenon and the misconceptions surrounding it. The significant thing about 1 Corinthians 12:9, 28 is that both gift and healing are plural and lack the definite article, hence the translation: "gifts of healings." Evidently Paul did not envision that a person would be endowed with one healing gift operative at all times for all diseases. His language suggests either many different gifts or powers of healing, each appropriate to and effective for its related illness, or each occurrence of healing constituting a distinct gift in its own right.

I've had the opportunity on numerous occasions to meet people who have what appears to be a healing anointing for one particular affliction. Some are able to pray more effectively for those with back problems while others see more success when praying for migraine headaches. This may be what Paul had in mind when he spoke of "gifts of healings."

One of the principal obstacles to a proper understanding of healing is the erroneous assumption that if anyone could *ever* heal, he could *always* heal. But in view of the lingering illness of

Epaphroditus (Phil. 2:25-30), Timothy (1 Tim. 5:23), Trophimus (2 Tim. 4:20), and perhaps Paul himself (2 Cor. 12:7-10; Gal. 4:13), it is better to view this gift as subject to the will of God, not the will of people. Therefore, a person may be gifted to heal many people, but not all. Another may be gifted to heal only one person at one particular time of one particular disease. When asked to pray for the sick, people are often heard to respond: "I can't. I don't have the gift of healing." But if my reading of Paul is correct, there is no such thing as *the* gift of healing, especially if it is envisioned as a God-given ability to heal everyone of every disease on every occasion. Rather, the Spirit sovereignly distributes a charisma of healing for a particular occasion, even though previous prayers for physical restoration under similar circumstances may not have been answered, and even though subsequent prayers for the same affliction may not be answered. In sum: "gifts of healings" are occasional and subject to the sovereign purposes of God.

Few doubt that Paul had a gift for healing, but his prayers for Epaphroditus weren't answered, at least not at first (Phil. 2: 25-30). Clearly, Paul could not heal at will. Aside from Jesus, no one else could either! And there is doubt if even Jesus could (John 5:19; Mark 6:5-6). Some would conclude from Paul's failure to heal his friend that the gift of healing was dying out at this juncture in the life of the church (in spite of the fact that late in his ministry, in Acts 28:9, Paul healed everyone on the island of Malta who came to him). It seems better to conclude that healing, whenever and wherever it occurred, was subject not to the will of man, but to the will of God. No one, not even Paul, could always heal all diseases. Paul understood the occasional nature of gifts of healings. If Paul was distressed that Epaphroditus was ill, almost unto death, and that initially his prayers for him were ineffective, I doubt seriously if the apostle would have drawn the same conclusions that modern cessationists do.

The fact that healing is an expression of divine mercy (Phil. 2:27) means that it should never be viewed as a right. Healing is not the payment of a debt. God does not owe us healing. We don't deserve healing. I believe we should have faith for healing. But there is a vast difference between faith in divine mercy and presumption based on an alleged right.

The word *mercy* is the same one used in the gospels to describe why Jesus healed people while he was on the earth. God's motive for healing hasn't changed! The primary reason God healed through Jesus prior to Pentecost was because he is a merciful, compassionate God. And the primary reason God continues to heal after Pentecost is because he is a merciful, compassionate God. God is no less merciful, no less compassionate, no less caring when it comes to the physical condition of his people after Pentecost than he was before Pentecost.

More Than a Spirit

One of the reasons some in the church today disregard healing is because they disregard the physical body. They believe that to focus on the health and well-being of the body (at least to the degree that you would regularly pray for its healing) is misguided. Our attention is to be more spiritual as we focus on the condition of our souls. This is little more than a modern version of ancient Gnosticism.

Among the many beliefs of ancient Gnosticism was that the physical body is not the creation of God. It was considered evil, as was all matter. They believed the body is a temporary prison-house of the soul, from which all of us will be delivered at death.

Gnostics tended to one of two extremes as a result of this belief. Some were inclined to deprive the body, to punish it, to treat it harshly through ascetic disciplines such as extended fasting and self-flagellation, while others went to the opposite extreme by indulging the body in all forms of sensual pleasure such as promiscuous sex and excessive food and drink.

The biblical view of the body, on the other hand, is quite positive. God created us as physical beings. We are both material and immaterial (see Gen. 2:7). The importance of the body is seen in the fact that our bodies were redeemed by the blood of Christ no less than our souls (1 Cor. 6:20). Our bodies are the temple of the Holy Spirit (1 Cor. 6:19). Our bodies are designed "for the Lord" (1 Cor. 6:13). Our bodies are members of Christ himself (1 Cor. 6:15). Our bodies are capable of being sinned against (1 Cor. 6:18). Our bodies are to be used to honor God (1 Cor. 6:20). Our bodies will be resurrected and glorified. In other words, we will spend eternity as *physically* glorified beings (see Rom. 8:11, 23; 1 Cor. 15:35-49). At the judgment seat of Christ we will have to give an account for what we have done in our bodies.

The Laying on of Hands

There is no escaping the fact that spirituality is physical. Although God is spirit, he created the physical, material world and pronounced it good (Gen. 1:4, 12, 18, 21, 25). When God created us in his image he gave us bodies.

These truths are nowhere better seen than in the biblical emphasis on "the laying on of hands." On several occasions Jesus healed people with the spoken word alone. But in most instances he did so by laying his hands on them or by touching or making physical contact.[5] Perhaps the most amazing text of all is Luke 4:40 where it is said that Jesus laid hands on "every one" of those in a vast multitude who had come to him for aid. It must have been physically exhausting and time-intensive for him to do so, but Jesus took the opportunity to lay his hands on every person who came to him for prayer.

Concluding Principles

Let me close with several important observations that I hope will encourage you to take your hands out of your pockets, fix your faith on the grace and power of God, and pray regularly for the sick.

First, healing and health are always portrayed in Scripture as the *blessing* of God. Nowhere in the Bible does God promise sickness or disease as blessings for his obedient children. Whereas it is true that God can use sickness to discipline and instruct us (see Ps. 6:2-3, 6-7; 32:1-7; 38; 41:1-4; 88:1-9, 15-18; 102: 1-5, 8-11; 119:67, 71, 75), sickness in and of itself is never portrayed as good.

Second, whereas all sickness is suffering, not all suffering is sickness. Jesus promised that all who follow him would suffer persecution, slander, rejection, and oppression. But he never said that about sickness. Nowhere in the Bible are obedient children of God told to expect sickness and disease as part of their calling in life. Sickness is not a part of the cross we are called to bear.

Third, contrary to popular thought, sickness and disease, in and of themselves, do not glorify God. Our unwavering faith and loyalty and love for God *in spite of* sickness and disease do glorify God.

Fourth, we must leave room for mystery in God's ways.

Some things will always remain unexplained. We can't always expect to understand why some are sick and others not, or why some are healed and others not. But most important of all, the fact that many, perhaps even most, are not healed should never be used to justify our disobedience to God's Word when it comes to praying for them.

Fifth, God's heart is for healing, not hurting. My working assumption is that God's heart is for healing unless I'm shown otherwise by divine revelation or death. What this means in practical terms is that you should continue to pray for the sick until God tells you otherwise or they die![6]

Sixth, we must be willing to bear the stigma of perceived failure. We have succeeded when we have obeyed the Scriptures to pray for the sick. Whether or not they are healed rests with God.

Many in the church today say they believe that God still heals, but they live as functional deists who rarely if ever actually lay hands on the sick and pray with any degree of expectancy. One reason is that they often confuse praying *expectantly* with praying *presumptuously*. Prayer is presumptuous when the person claims healing without revelatory warrant or on the unbiblical assumption that God always wills to heal then and there. They then feel required to account for the absence of healing by appealing either to moral failure or deficiency of faith (usually in the one for whom prayer is offered).

People pray expectantly when they humbly petition a merciful God for something they don't deserve but that he delights to give (Luke 11:9-13; cf. Matt. 9:27-31; 20:29-34; Luke 17:13-14). Expectant prayer flows from the recognition that Jesus healed people because he loved them and felt compassion for them (Matt. 14:13-14; 20:34; Mark 1:41-42; Luke 7: 11-17), a disposition in the heart of God that nothing in Scripture indicates has changed.

FIVE

It's a Miracle!

Is it OK to pray for a miracle? For many years I thought it was unspiritual to desire or seek after any spiritual gifts, especially those of a more overt miraculous nature. I had been taught it was an indication of immaturity to seek signs in any sense, that it was a weak faith, born of theological ignorance, that prayed for healing or a demonstration of divine power. One author I read actually said that to desire miracles is sinful and unbelieving! But then I noticed Acts 4:29-31, which records this prayer of the church in Jerusalem:

> "And now, Lord, take note of their threats, and grant that Thy bond-servants may speak Thy word with all confidence, while Thou dost extend Thy hand to heal, and signs and wonders take place through the name of Thy holy servant Jesus." And when they had prayed, the place where they had gathered together was shaken, and they were all filled with the Holy Spirit, and began to speak the word of God with boldness.

I trust that no one would accuse these believers of emotionalism or mental imbalance! Evidently they didn't believe there was any inconsistency between miracles and the message of the gospel, between the wonders for which they prayed and the word of the cross they so fervently preached.

But didn't Jesus rebuke as wicked and adulterous those who "crave" and "seek" after signs (Matt. 12:39; 16:4; compare with 1 Cor. 1:22)? Yes, but the people he denounced were unbelieving scribes and Pharisees, not Christians. These people were desperate for a way to justify their unbelief and rationalize their refusal to follow Jesus. There's no reason why their motivation for seeking signs should be yours or mine.

If our prayers for power are born of a desire to see God glorified and his people healed, I hardly think Jesus would respond to us as he did the religious leaders of his day. When a passion for miraculous gifts is prompted not by a selfish hankering for the sensational, but by compassion for diseased and despairing souls, God cannot but be pleased.

Doing the Works of Jesus

One of the most amazing things Jesus ever said is found in John 14:12: "Truly, truly, I say to you, he who believes in Me the works that I do shall he do also; and greater works than these shall he do; because I go to the Father." Virtually everyone is confused, to some degree, by this text. The question is: How do you respond to your confusion? It seems there are only three options.

Some simply reject the text and figure out how to live with a Bible that contains error. I seriously doubt if many who read this book would adopt such a viewpoint.

The majority of people I know interpret the text in the light of their inability to explain how their experience does not measure up to its claims. This was the position I embraced for a number of years. But in good conscience, I can do so no longer.

The third option is to receive the text and trust God to sort out the confusion as we seek to pray for its fulfillment.

Many have attempted to explain Jesus' words as referring to something other than miraculous deeds and physical healing.

For example, some have argued that Jesus' followers would do a greater *number* of works than Jesus did (due to the fact that the church is a multitude whereas Jesus is but one). But this is so patently obvious that it hardly seems necessary for Jesus to assert it.

Others contend that the greater works Jesus' followers were to do was a reference to evangelistic success in the number of souls saved. After all, whereas Jesus accomplished much in his earthly ministry, the number of people who came to saving faith while in his physical presence was quite small. Another interpretation appeals to Matthew 11:11 where Jesus said that the "least in the kingdom of heaven is greater than he [referring to John the Baptist]." As great as John was, he never experienced the fullness of the blessings of the kingdom of heaven that came through the death—and especially the resurrection—of Jesus. John's ministry came too early in redemptive history to permit him to participate in the glory of the new age, which Jesus inaugurated. Thus, it is argued, the works performed after Jesus ascends and sends the Spirit are greater since they will occur in a different and more advanced phase of God's plan of salvation, being based on Jesus' finished work of redemption.

There are three problems with all of the preceding interpretations. First, Jesus described a person who performed these works as "he who believes in me." This particular Greek phrase in John's Gospel always refers to all believers, to any person who trusts in Christ, whether apostle or average follower (see John 3:15-16, 18, 36; 6:35, 40, 47; 7:38; 11:25-26; 12:44, 46; 14:12). This descriptive phrase never refers to a select group within the larger body of Christ. It never refers solely to the apostles. Therefore, any attempt to restrict the fulfillment of John 14:12 to a narrow group of special saints who have long since died simply won't work.

Second, the works believers are said to perform may well be *more than* miraculous deeds and physical healings, but they are certainly *not less than* miraculous deeds and healings. The immediately preceding verse says: "Believe Me that I am in the Father, and the Father in Me; otherwise believe on account of the works themselves" (John 14:11). If one was to believe in Jesus "on account of" certain "works" that he did, that is to say, if certain works were to serve as a basis or ground for faith, they must have been visible and unavoidable. Those works on account of which Jesus consistently called people to believe were the miracles he performed.[1]

My third problem with these interpretations is that most people focus on the greater works in the second half of verse 12 and fail to address the *equivalent works* in the first half of the verse. Even if one were able to explain away the greater works as something other than miracles (such as evangelistic success), one must still explain the fact that Jesus promised that those who believed him would do the *same* works he did.

Jesus attributed the ability of his followers to do his works to the fact that he was going "to the Father." In the context of the Upper Room discourse (John 13–17) this clearly points us to the gift of the Holy Spirit that was dependent on Jesus' ascension to the Father's right hand (see John 14:16, 26; 15:26; 16:7).

Finally, if the works Jesus did and promised that believers would do were a reference to miraculous deeds and physical healings, is it not likely that the complete fulfillment of this word is yet future? If what Jesus said is true, and *everything* he said is true, then surely this promise has yet to see its consummate fulfillment. Could it be that it will happen in our generation?

The Gift of Miracles

The most literal translation of Paul's words in 1 Corinthians 12:10 is "workings of powers" (*energēmata dunameōn*). Although all gifts are "workings" (*energēmata*) or "energizings" by divine power (compare with vv. 6, 11), the word is used here in conjunction with "powers" (*dunamis*) for a particular gift. The word often translated "miracles" in 1 Corinthians 12:10 is actually the Greek word for powers (*dunamis*). Thus we again have a double plural, "workings of powers," which probably points to a certain variety in these operations.

What are these "workings" or "effectings" or "productions" of "powers"? It seems unlikely that Paul would include healing in the exercise of this gift. That isn't to say that healing isn't a miracle. Rather, it's simply to say that Paul would not unnecessarily repeat himself. Whereas healings are certainly miraculous, the gift of miracles must primarily encompass other supernatural phenomena as well. Simply put, whereas all healings are displays of power, not all displays of power are healings.

Several possible manifestations of divine power may be included in what Paul means by "workings of powers" or "miracles." Consider the following:

- See Acts 9:40 where Peter raised Tabitha/Dorcas from the dead (although even this is a healing in the strictest sense of the term).
- See Acts 13:8-11 where Paul induced blindness on Elymas. One might also include here Peter's word of disciplinary judgment that resulted in the immediate death of Ananias and Sapphira (Acts 5:1-11).
- Perhaps nature miracles would be included here, such as turning water to wine, stilling the storm on the Sea of

Galilee, reproducing food, and causing the rain to cease (or commence), as with Elijah.

- Perhaps supernatural deliverances (exorcisms) are in view as well.

Defining a Miracle

The word *miracle* is used somewhat promiscuously to describe everything from healing a paralytic to finding a parking space at the mall on the day before Christmas. What is a good, biblical, working definition of a miracle? Max Turner, a professor of New Testament at London Bible College, uses the term in the semi-technical sense of an event that combines the following traits:

(1) it is an extraordinary or startling observable event, (2) it cannot reasonably be explained in terms of human abilities or other known forces in the world, (3) it is perceived as a direct act of God, and (4) it is usually understood to have symbolic or sign value (e.g., pointing to God as redeemer and judge).[2]

Part of the problem is that many Christians envision God as remote from the world, removed from any direct involvement in their lives on a daily basis. Yet there are numerous texts that assert God's immediate involvement in everything from the growth of a blade of grass (Ps. 104) to the sustaining of our very lives (Acts 17; Col. 1:17). For this reason we must reject the definition of a miracle as a direct intervention of God into the world. The phrase "intervention ... into" implies that God is outside the world and only occasionally intrudes in its affairs. Some define a miracle as God working in the world apart from means, or an instrument, that would bring about the desired result. But God often uses instruments in performing the miraculous, as in the case of Jesus' feeding of the five thousand by means of multiplying one little boy's lunch.

Others define a miracle as God acting contrary to natural law. But this implies there are forces (natural laws) that operate independently of God, forces or laws that God must violate or override to perform a miracle. But God is the author and providential Lord over all natural processes.

Grudem has proposed a definition that avoids the virus of deism while seeking to remain faithful to the Scriptures: "A miracle," says Grudem, "is a less common kind of God's activity in which he arouses people's awe and wonder and bears witness to himself."[3] What's important for us to remember is that no matter how we define a miracle, we must not think that a miracle means a typically absent God is now present. Rather, the God who is always and everywhere present, upholding and sustaining and directing all things to their appointed consummation, is now working in a surprising and unfamiliar way. This also helps us answer the question of whether unusual answers to prayer are miracles. I would say yes—*if* such answers are sufficiently unusual to arouse awe and wonder and to evoke acknowledgment of God's power and activity (e.g., 1 Kings 18:24, 36-38; Acts 12:5-17; 28:8).

Was Jesus a "Reluctant" Miracle-Worker?

One reason people are reluctant to pray for a miracle, much less the gift of miracles, is that they think Jesus was reluctant, too. Philip Yancey, author of such popular books as *Disappointment With God* and *Where Is God When It Hurts?*, suggests that miracles played a far less significant role in Jesus' ministry than we have been led to believe.[4] Yancey made much the same point in his book *The Jesus I Never Knew*.

I agree with a few of Yancey's statements about Jesus, one of which is his observation that "Jesus did no miracles for the purposes of fund-raising, fame, or self-protection." In an article in a popular Christian magazine he makes ten points showing that Jesus was a reluctant miracle worker, several of which I find misleading and in need of correction. I've combined my response to them under five headings. Please note, however, that I have the utmost respect for Yancey and his writings. I'm using his comments simply because they accurately embody what I fear many evangelicals believe about miracles—beliefs that I think we should carefully reconsider.

(1) Yancey wrote:

The Gospels record about three dozen miracles, some of them group healings. (Many other miracles performed by Jesus, John tells us, are not recorded.) Although very impressive to eyewitnesses, the miracles affected a relatively small number of people who lived in one tiny corner of the world. No Europeans or Chinese felt Jesus' healing touch. Clearly, he did not come to solve "the problem of pain" while on earth.[5]

I'm concerned about the implications of this statement. Yancey evidently believes that "three dozen miracles" is a small number, the implication being that miracles were therefore comparatively unimportant to Jesus himself and therefore ought to be comparatively unimportant to us today. But when one considers the nature of these approximately thirty-six miracles, quite a different conclusion is called for: raising people from the dead, instantaneously cleansing lepers, healing people born paralyzed, giving sight to those totally blind, walking on water, reproducing fish and bread to feed thousands, and the list could go on.

Yancey conceded that some of these miracles were "group healings," but do you realize what that means? Take Matthew 4 and Luke 4 where we read that "great multitudes" came with people suffering from "every kind of sickness." It is reasonable to estimate that several hundred (if not thousand) people were present at these gatherings at which Jesus healed "everyone"! This hardly leads to the conclusion that he performed only around "three dozen miracles" and that such activity was therefore a comparatively unimportant part of his ministry.

In a parenthetical statement, Yancey appears to dismiss the statements in John 20:30 and 21:25 regarding unrecorded acts of Jesus. The fact is that these verses say Jesus performed so "many" (John 21:25) more miracles than what are recorded in Scripture that it would be difficult for them all to be numbered. When all is said and done, although no one can be precise, I would suggest that in the course of his three-year public ministry Jesus performed *several thousand* miracles, which is a far cry from "three dozen"!

Yancey thinks it significant that these miracles only affected a relatively small number of people. But what else could one expect, given the fact that Jesus only lived and ministered in Palestine, not in Europe or China or elsewhere? To suggest that his miracles weren't an important part of his ministry simply because people in China didn't feel his personal touch is a bit misleading. Indeed, I dare say that people in China today are being profoundly touched and impacted by the miracle-working Christ, as the reports of revival and supernatural phenomena there continue to reach Western ears.

Yancey concluded that Jesus "did not come to solve 'the problem of pain' while on earth." Yet, Jesus described the purpose of his ministry as "preach[ing] the gospel to the poor" and "proclaim[ing] release to the captives" and bringing "recovery of sight to the blind" and setting free "those who are downtrodden" (Luke 4:18). My guess is that people suffering in poverty and in prison and from physical illness and broken hearts would also have a different opinion. If Yancey meant that Jesus did not come to immediately eradicate pain from the earth, he's right. But Jesus most certainly *did* come to solve the problem of pain, and that in three ways.

First, his personal ministry focused on delivering individuals from pain and poverty and demons and distress. Second, his death on the cross is the foundation for the ultimate removal of pain from his people, whether that happens now or in heaven. The fact is, though, that is why he came. Third, Jesus ascended to heaven in order that he might send the Spirit so that we might do the very works of healing and deliverance and mercy and miracles that he himself did (John 14:12).

I'm not saying that all pain will disappear prior to Christ's return. But even then, Jesus came to give us an example of how to bear up under it (see 2 Cor. 12 and Paul's "thorn in the flesh"), if not to be healed and delivered from it. We should pray for healing and deliverance from pain, confident that our loving heavenly Father delights in glorifying his Son by ministering to us in mercy and compassion. But if for reasons beyond our understanding the Father chooses instead to give us grace and strength to endure pain as we await his Son from heaven, so be it. In either case, it is simplistic to say that Jesus did not come to solve the problem of pain. For if Jesus didn't, who will? Indeed, who can?

(2) Yancey argued that Jesus resisted miracles "on demand" and pointed to his rebuke of those who asked for a miraculous sign. Related to this is Yancey's appeal to Jesus' instruction to his disciples not to tell people about certain miracles ostensibly because Jesus "seemed wary of the kind of faith miracles may produce" (namely, "an attraction for show or for magic, not the kind of sacrificial lifelong commitment he required"). This leaves the unsuspecting reader with the impression that to pray for a miracle is sinful, or at least a sign of immaturity, and that miracles produce substandard faith. Let me simply refer you to my response to this point in chapter one.

Many Christians are confused about how miracles relate to the gospel of Christ crucified. They are afraid that prayer for the former entails neglect of the latter. Such fears are unfounded. I believe in the absolute centrality of the cross of Christ and its power to save lost souls (Rom. 1:16). Quite obviously, so did Paul, a man who described his gospel ministry as one characterized by the "power of signs and wonders, in the power of the [Holy] Spirit" (Rom. 15:19). The same man who declared that "the word of the cross" is the power of God to salvation (1 Cor. 1:18) also wrote 1 Corinthians 12–14! The same man who pronounced *anathema* (Gal. 1:6-8) on any who tampered with the gospel is the central figure in the book of Acts with all its miraculous phenomena. The same man who said, "I determined to know nothing among you except Jesus Christ, and Him crucified" (1 Cor. 2:2), also preached that truth "not in persuasive words of wisdom, but in demonstration of the Spirit and of power" (1 Cor. 2:4). It was this same Paul who reminded the Thessalonians that the gospel did not come to them "in word only, but also in power and in the Holy Spirit and with full conviction" (1 Thess. 1:5).

If that weren't enough, God himself is described as "bearing witness to the word of His grace, granting that signs and wonders be done by their hands" (Acts 14:3). Surely God is not guilty of inconsistency or of undermining his own activity! I can only conclude that if there is a conflict between miraculous activity of the Spirit and the word of the cross, it is in *our* minds that the problem exists. It wasn't in Paul's mind. And it certainly isn't in God's.

Others have argued that any focus on the power of spiritual gifts will breed a spirit of triumphalism inconsistent with the call to suffer for the sake of the gospel. Those who desire and pray for the miraculous, so goes the charge, do not take seriously the painful realities of living in a fallen world. I certainly agree that weakness, afflictions, persecution, and suffering are an inevitable part of living in the "not-yet" of the kingdom, but this need not entail a diminished emphasis on the charismata. Paul certainly sensed no incompatibility between the two, for they were both characteristic of his life and ministry. The miracles in the ministry of Paul were not performed from a platform, elevated above the rigors of life or insulated from the pains of persecution, but rather in the midst of the distress and slander and heartache that he invariably suffered as an obedient servant of Christ.

As John Piper has said, "Paul's 'thorn' [in the flesh] no doubt pressed deeper with every healing he performed."[5] Personal trials and afflictions did not lead him to renounce the miraculous in his ministry. Nor did the supernatural displays of God's power lead him into a naive, Pollyanna-like outlook on the human condition. Again, if signs and suffering are incompatible, one must look somewhere other than in the Bible to prove it.

(3) Although I noted this above, I want to say something more about Yancey's suggestion that "the kind of faith miracles

may produce" is not mature or sufficient to enable us to make lifelong sacrifices in following Christ.[6] Miracles do not always produce saving faith in those who witness them, but that is not because of something at fault in the miracle or because miracles are inherently dangerous or any such notion. It is simply because people are extremely hardhearted and calloused and spiritually blind. But that is no reason not to pray for or expect miracles. The fact is, miracles often lead to great evangelistic success (John 5:36; 10:25, 37-38; 12:9-11; 14:11; 20:30-31; Acts 8:4-8; 9:32-43; Rom. 15:18-19) and can be a tremendous boost to our faith in the power and compassion of God (1 Cor. 14:3 and other texts). By the way, I find it instructive that the apostle Paul believed that supernatural phenomena such as healings, tongues, prophecy, and even the gift of *miracles* were all given by God to the church "for the common good" (1 Cor. 12:7)!

(4) Yancey wrote, "Spectacular miracles created distance, not intimacy," and pointed to the disciples' reaction when Jesus calmed the storm on the Sea of Galilee. This leads the undiscerning reader to think that he or she should not pray for or expect miracles because such phenomena not only fail to engender intimacy with God, they also hinder it. After all, who wants "distance" from God? If you want "intimacy," stay away from miracles. Perhaps Yancey would not want me to draw such conclusions, but both the way he phrased his statement and the absence of important qualifying and nuanced explanations of what it does *not* mean can only mislead the average Christian reader and create an unconscious and ill-informed prejudice against the supernatural.

(5) Yancey asserted that "spiritual miracles tended to excite Jesus more than physical ones." I agree with this, if by spiritual

miracles he means the miracle of conversion and the like. But that does *not* mean or imply that physical miracles are unimportant or to be avoided or somehow off-limits to believers who stand in need of God's power. Yancey then appealed to the healing of the paralytic where Jesus asked the Pharisees, "Which is easier, to say to the paralytic, 'Your sins are forgiven,' or to say, 'Get up, take your mat, and walk'?" Yancey's answer was: "Physical healing was far easier." But I'm not so sure.

I think it is easier to speak the words, "Your sins are forgiven," because no man knows whether or not they are. It is much harder to say, "Rise and walk," because observers can immediately verify or falsify the statement by looking to see whether or not the paralyzed person walks. Jesus' point was to prove that he had the power to forgive sins (something invisible) by demonstrating the power to heal the lame (something visible). Jesus himself then declared: "But in order that you may know that the Son of Man has authority on earth to forgive sins ... I say to you, rise, take up your pallet and go home" (Mark 2:10-11). This is simply one example of the challenge issued by Jesus to the Pharisees in John 10:

> If I do not do the works of My Father, do not believe Me; but if I do them, though you do not believe Me, believe the works, that you may know and understand that the Father is in Me, and I in the Father.
>
> JOHN 10:37-38

Are miracles the cure-all for society's ills and the church's problems? Of course not. Jesus is. But the Jesus who entered society and ministered to its ills, the Jesus who created the church and is its sovereign, saving Lord, is *a miracle-working Jesus*. And I do not believe he was, or is, at all reluctant to be described as such. And if God should graciously equip us to minister in the miraculous, neither should we be.

Two Examples

As I've noted, the gift of miracles, or "powers," probably refers to displays of supernatural power other than physical healing (although the latter is itself miraculous in nature). Let me give you two examples. They both occurred in the early days of the church in Kansas City where I served as an associate pastor for seven years.

On Wednesday night, April 13 of 1983, senior pastor Mike Bickle sensed the Lord leading him to call a church-wide, twenty-one-day fast to pray for God's purposes in the city. Mike decided the fast was to begin on May 7. The next day a prophetically gifted man named Bob Jones told Mike that God would confirm this revelation by sending a sign in the heavens that could not be the product of human engineering. Bob said:

God is going to send a comet in the heavens that as of today no scientist or astronomer anywhere in the world has discovered or predicted. It will come as a complete surprise to them and will prove beyond a shadow of a doubt that God has called this time of prayer and fasting and that he fully intends to bring revival to this city and country.

Stop and catch your breath for a moment and think of the implications of this word. This was a pretty bold statement. This wasn't the interpretation of someone's dream or advice on how to know God's will or assurance to a distraught believer that his non-Christian wife would soon come to faith. Here was an unequivocal, unabashed prediction of a comet unknown to the scientific community. There isn't much chance here for sleight of hand or religious trickery or other well-known tactics of palm readers and psychics.

Mike had called for the fast to begin on May 7, 1983. He had informed Bob Jones of this on the morning of April 14. Bob prophesied the appearance of the comet on that same day. I can hear the rumblings of the skeptic: "But what if Bob Jones secretly found out about this comet *before* he and Mike talked on the fourteenth? He could then easily pass off this information as a prophetic word just to enhance his ministry and magnify his status in the church."

Sure, he could have. But there is one problem. The comet wasn't discovered for another *eleven days!* Comet IRAS-Araki-Alcock was first discovered in data relayed to earth on April 25 by the Infra Red Astronomical Satellite (known as IRAS) and then independently confirmed by two amateur astronomers, a man named Genichi Araki in Japan and another named G.E.D. Alcock in England, who saw it with binoculars from his window. Although it was not an extremely large comet, it came closer to earth than any comet in over two hundred years and remains the second closest encounter in history.[7]

When May 7 arrived and the fast was to begin, numerous pastors from other churches in the city were present. Mike had each of them introduce themselves at the beginning of the meeting. But the most exciting moment of that day came when Bob Jones walked in with that day's edition of *The Independence (Missouri) Examiner*. News of the comet had finally reached the newspapers. The headline read: "Comet's Pass to Give Close View." The article went on to report:

Scientists will have a rare chance next week to study a recently discovered comet that is coming within the "extremely" close range of 3 million miles.... Dr. Gerry Neugebauer, principal U.S. investigator on the international Infrared Astronomical Satellite Project (IRAS) said, "... It was sheer good luck we happened to be looking where the comet was passing."

In a recent book, author and astronomer Fred Schaff again commented on "the suddenness of this object's arrival."[8] In virtually every written account of the comet, reference is made to the sudden and unexpected nature of its coming. Phrases such as "newly discovered" and "surprise appearance" are repeatedly used.

With such a spectacular start, there were high expectations for the twenty-one-day fast. But on the final day of the fast, Bob Jones delivered what had to have been a disconcerting word.

The Lord spoke to me in a dream last night and said that revival will not begin immediately as we had thought. God will withhold his move upon this city until the appointed time and season. And when it comes it will not be a day late.

This was not good news to those who had been fasting, many on water only, for the last twenty-one days. But Bob wasn't finished.

God is going to send yet another sign. There will be a three-month drought in the natural over this city, even as there will be a three-month drought in the Spirit. But on August 23 it will rain as a sign to you that in God's time he will send the rain of the Spirit even as he has promised.

The drought began at the end of June and extended into the first week of October, just as Bob said it would. In fact, those three months in 1983 proved to be the second driest summer in Kansas City in more than one hundred years![9] But what about August 23? I was hoping you hadn't forgotten.

As of the twenty-second of August, Kansas City had received only .21 inches of rain for the entire month. Normal rainfall for this same period was 2.36 inches. The church was scheduled to have a meeting August 23, even though the weather reports insisted that no rain was in sight. People's nerves were on edge. What if it didn't rain? It seemed as if everything was on the line: the validity of prophetic ministry, the purpose of the May fast, the credibility of both Mike and Bob. By evening, however, rain clouds had formed. When the heavens burst open and a torrential rain (.32 of an inch in less than an hour) fell upon that small group of believers, they knew that God had spoken. Many ran from the parking lot shouting with joy, drenched from head to foot. The next day the drought resumed and continued unabated until its appointed time was fulfilled that autumn.

By the way, you may find it interesting, as I did, that on the front page of the *Kansas City Star* newspaper on the morning of the twenty-fourth was a picture taken the day before of a lady sitting beneath her umbrella with a fishing pole in hand. The caption read, "Just fishing in the rain." The article went on to describe how the rain showers of the twenty-third provided only a temporary break from the brutally hot and dry weather.

Miracles are by definition unusual and extraordinary events. They are not daily events that we can predict or expect with regularity. But we must not let that deter us from praying for the manifestation of God's supernatural power or in any way diminish the reality of this particular spiritual gift.

SIX

Prophecy and Distinguishing of Spirits

A former student of mine was going through a difficult season in her life. God seemed far away. Her job was unfulfilling. She thought about quitting and pursuing a different line of work. She certainly didn't expect what happened next.

It was at a conference in the summer of 1994 where more than 2,000 people were in attendance. Although he had never met her before, a man widely known for his prophetic gift asked this student to stand. As he was giving her words of encouragement, together with some advice drawn from a biblical text he thought was relevant to her life, he paused and said: "I just saw the number *202* above your head. I believe that is where you work." He then resumed delivery of the word.

I was closely watching this lady while he was speaking. I noticed her initial confusion when he mentioned 202 and then, about thirty seconds later, her sudden realization of what he had said. I later asked her what happened. She said, "When he identified 202 as the place I worked, I mistakenly thought he was giving the street address. My first reaction was that he had missed it. But a few moments later it dawned on me that 202 is the number of my office suite in the downtown building where I work!"

I've seen this sort of thing dozens of times. A prophetic word seems so often to come at just the right time in a person's life, at that moment when there is a need to know that God is near, that he cares, that he still loves and guides and answers prayer. What are we to make of it? There is simply no possible way to explain this phenomenon as a lucky guess or coincidence. The information either came from the devil to deceive and destroy my student's confidence in God, or it came from the Holy Spirit to "edify, exhort, and console" her (1 Cor. 14:3).

When I use the word *prophecy* I am not referring primarily to the prediction of future events. Unfortunately, the word has come to be associated almost exclusively in the minds of many with what they might read in one of Hal Lindsey's books on the end times. But when I use the word *prophecy*, I have in mind the spiritual gift described by Paul in 1 Corinthians 12–14 and elsewhere in the New Testament. A simple definition would be that prophecy is "the human report of a divine revelation." Prophecy is the speaking forth in merely human words of something God has spontaneously brought to mind.

Much has been written on this subject, but I want to take a slightly different approach. In all our talk of prophecy and the many stories we tell, there is a tendency to neglect the principles and guidelines for this gift set forth by the apostle Paul in 1 Corinthians 14. I believe much of the confusion as well as the errors into which people often fall through misuse of this gift could be dispelled if we would only take the time to carefully examine all that Paul says in this important chapter of the New Testament. Therefore, I want to take you on a short study of 1 Corinthians 14. Again, I encourage you to read this discussion with an open Bible. What follows is not a verse-by-verse exposition of 1 Corinthians 14 but rather selected insights that seek to answer several crucial questions about the nature and function of the prophetic gift.

Is It OK to Pursue Prophecy?

Not only is it OK, it's mandatory. In 1 Corinthians 14:1 Paul commanded us to desire earnestly spiritual gifts, "especially that you may prophesy." Again in 1 Corinthians 14:39 Paul exhorted us to "desire earnestly to prophesy." In 14:12 Paul wrote, "So also you, since you are zealous of spiritual gifts [referring to his readers' collective enthusiasm for tongues], seek to abound for the edification of the church [in particular, the gift of prophecy, according to the context]."

This is truly an astounding statement. Paul was not merely suggesting that prophecy is a good gift. He was commanding that we earnestly desire to exercise this gift in the local body. This is not an option. Paul did not give us a choice. His words leave us little room for maneuvering. The point is: If you are not earnestly desiring to prophesy, if you are not praying for opportunity and occasion to speak prophetically into the lives of the church and other believers, you are disobeying God! The pursuit of prophecy is a moral and spiritual obligation to which we must devote ourselves.

Can Anyone Prophesy?

Yes, *any* believer could prophesy, but that doesn't mean *every* believer should expect to function consistently as a prophet in the church. Paul wished that "all" would prophesy (1 Cor. 14:5), but does that mean he *expected* them to? His desire for people to prophesy came from his recognition that the "one who prophesies edifies the church" (1 Cor. 14:4). In two other texts he seemed to envision the possibility that any Christian might speak prophetically (1 Cor. 14:24, 31). But again this doesn't mean that everyone *will*. Paul was probably drawing a distinction between persons who consistently display a facility and accuracy in prophecy and those who merely prophesy on occasion.

We must also keep in mind Peter's quotation in Acts 2 of Joel's prophecy concerning the outpouring of the Spirit. The result of this effusion of the Spirit is that "your sons and your daughters shall prophesy" (Acts 2:17). The characteristic feature of this present church age is the revelatory activity of the Spirit (dreams and visions), which forms the basis for prophetic utterance. Not all will be prophets (Eph. 4:11; 1 Cor. 12:29), but it would appear that all *may* prophesy.

What Information Does God Disclose in Prophecy?

In 1 Corinthians 14:25 Paul described prophecy as disclosing the "secrets" of the heart. On numerous occasions I have witnessed this phenomenon. Men and women who believed their thoughts, their fantasies, their sins, and their plans for the future were secretly hidden, even from God, were shocked by the revelatory activity of the Spirit. Paul describes only one of the many ways a person might respond to the prophetic gift: "he will fall on his face and worship God, declaring that God is certainly among you" (v. 25).

I referred earlier to Charles Spurgeon (1834–92), widely regarded as one of the greatest preachers the church has ever known. His life was an irreproachable example of godliness and zeal, and his ministry was characterized by an unfailing commitment to the authority of Scripture. Thousands bear witness to the impact of Spurgeon on their lives.

Although Spurgeon deeply loved and depended on the

power of the Holy Spirit in his ministry, he was not known for advocating the validity of miraculous gifts in the church. Yet Spurgeon himself experienced what can only be regarded as prophetic revelation. The fact that he did not refer to the experience as charismatic does not change the reality of what occurred in his pulpit. The following incidents are taken directly from Spurgeon's autobiography. You be the judge of whether or not they are expressions of the miraculous gifting described by the apostle Paul in 1 Corinthians 14:24-25.

While preaching in the hall, on one occasion, I deliberately pointed to a man in the midst of the crowd, and said, "There is a man sitting there, who is a shoemaker; he keeps his shop open on Sundays, it was open last Sabbath morning, he took ninepence, and there was fourpence profit out of it; his soul is sold to Satan for fourpence!" A city missionary, when going his rounds, met with this man, and seeing that he was reading one of my sermons, he asked the question, "Do you know Mr. Spurgeon?" "Yes," replied the man, "I have every reason to know him, I have been to hear him; and, under his preaching, by God's grace I have become a new creature in Christ Jesus. Shall I tell you how it happened? I went to the Music Hall, and took my seat in the middle of the place; Mr. Spurgeon looked at me as if he knew me, and in his sermon he pointed to me, and told the congregation that I was a shoemaker, and that I kept my shop open on Sundays; and I did, sir. I should not have minded that; but he also said that I took ninepence the Sunday before, and that there was fourpence profit out of it. I did take ninepence that day, and fourpence was just the profit; but how he should know that, I could not tell. Then it struck me that it was

God who had spoken to my soul through him, so I shut up my shop the next Sunday. At first, I was afraid to go again to hear him, lest he should tell the people more about me; but afterwards I went, and the Lord met with me, and saved my soul.'"[1]

Spurgeon then added this comment:

I could tell as many as a dozen similar cases in which I pointed at somebody in the hall without having the slightest knowledge of the person, or any idea that what I said was right, except that I believed I was moved by the Spirit to say it; and so striking has been my description, that the persons have gone away, and said to their friends, "Come, see a man that told me all things that ever I did; beyond a doubt, he must have been sent of God to my soul, or else he could not have described me so exactly." And not only so, but I have known many instances in which the thoughts of men have been revealed from the pulpit. I have sometimes seen persons nudge their neighbours with their elbow, because they had got a smart hit, and they have been heard to say, when they were going out, "The preacher told us just what we said to one another when we went in at the door."[2]

If one were to examine Spurgeon's theology and ministry, as well as recorded accounts of it by his contemporaries and subsequent biographers, you would find an absence of explicit reference to miraculous charismata such as prophecy and the word of knowledge. As a result, you would be tempted to conclude that such gifts had been withdrawn from church life. But Spurgeon's own testimony inadvertently says otherwise!

Where Does Prophecy Come From?

All prophecy is based on revelation. In 1 Corinthians 14:30 Paul wrote, "If a *revelation* is made to another who is seated, let the first keep silent" (emphasis added, see also v. 26). In 13:2 Paul seems to suggest that prophecies are based on the reception of divine "mysteries." The verb *to reveal* (*apokaluptō*) occurs twenty-six times in the New Testament, and the noun *revelation* occurs eighteen times. In every instance the reference is to divine activity, never to human communication.

Prophecy is not based on a hunch, a supposition, an inference, an educated guess, or even on sanctified wisdom. Prophecy is not based on personal insight, intuition, or illumination. Prophecy is the human *report* of a divine *revelation*. This is what distinguishes prophecy from teaching. Teaching is always based on a text of Scripture. Prophecy is always based on a spontaneous revelation.

Although rooted in revelation, prophecy is occasionally fallible. I know what you're thinking: "How can God reveal something that contains error? How can God, who is *infallible,* reveal something that is *fallible?*" The answer is simple: He can't. He doesn't.

We must remember that every prophecy has three elements, only one of which is assuredly of God. First, there is the *revelation* itself, the divine act of disclosure to a human recipient. The second element is the *interpretation* of what has been disclosed, or the attempt to ascertain its meaning. Third, there is the *application* of that interpretation. God is alone responsible for the revelation. Whatever he discloses to the human mind is wholly free from error. It is as infallible as God is. It is true in all its parts, completely devoid of falsehood. Indeed, the revelation, which is the root of every genuine prophetic utterance, is as inerrant and infallible as the written Word of God itself (the Bible).

The problem is that you might misinterpret or misapply what God has disclosed. The fact that God has *spoken* perfectly doesn't mean that you have *heard* perfectly. It is possible for a person to interpret and apply, without error, what God has revealed. But the mere existence of a divine revelation does not in itself guarantee that the interpretation or application of God's revealed truth will share in its perfection.

This is especially troubling to some and has led them to conclude that New Testament prophecy is of no benefit to the church. After all, how can a gift that is potentially fallible be a blessing to anyone? A comparison of prophecy with the gift of teaching should put your fears to rest.

Prophecy and Teaching

Consider this hypothetical, but not uncommon, scenario. The pastor of your church is teaching a series on the book of 1 Thessalonians. Each week in the pulpit he has before him the revealed, inspired, written Word of God, from which he draws (I hope) his comments. He has come to chapter four where Paul discusses the rapture of the church. He tells you that, after careful study and much prayer, he believes the rapture will occur before the tribulation.

After church you're having lunch with a friend who insists the rapture occurs at the midpoint of the tribulation. You, on the other hand, are no less persuaded that the rapture won't come until after the tribulation. What's going on? All three of you are reading the same Bible (even the same translation). Each of you has been diligent in studying the passage in question. Each of you has prayed for divine illumination. Yet, notwithstanding the presence of the objective, written revelation of God, you walk away with conflicting interpretations and differing applications of its relevance for your life. We might wish that God had promised to guarantee that our interpretation and subsequent communication of his revealed Word would always be accurate. But he didn't.

What should you do? Should you denounce teaching and insist that a gift so obviously susceptible to error and abuse be banned from church life? Of course not. In fact, you've been tremendously blessed by the series of sermons on Thessalonians and are excited about what God is doing in your own life. You realize that only the Bible has intrinsic divine authority. What your pastor says, in the exercise of his spiritual gift, has authority only in a secondary, derivative sense. Simply because he may have come up short in his interpretive and homiletical skills is no reason to repudiate the spiritual gift of teaching.

Like teaching, prophecy is also based on a revelation from God. In some way beyond ordinary sense perception, God *reveals* something to the mind of the prophet not found in Scripture (but never contrary to it). The revelation, having come from God, is true. It is error-free. Like the Bible, it alone has intrinsic divine authority. But the gift of prophecy does not guarantee the infallible *transmission* of that revelation. The prophet may *perceive* imperfectly, she may *understand* imperfectly, and, as a consequence, she may *communicate* imperfectly (not unlike what happened with your pastor and his exposition of 1 Thessalonians 4).

That is why Paul says we see in a mirror dimly (1 Cor. 13:12). The gift of prophecy may result in *fallible* prophecy just as the gift of teaching may result in *fallible* teaching. Therefore, if teaching (a gift prone to fallibility) can edify and build up the church, why can't prophecy be good for edifying as well (see 1 Cor. 14:3, 12, 26), even though both gifts suffer from human imperfection and stand in need of testing? (Precisely how this testing should be done is the focus of our next chapter.)

In What Form Does Revelation Come?

The form or manner in which the revelation comes is not specified. Whereas audible voice and vision are not ruled out, the revelation often comes in the form of words, thoughts, or perhaps mental pictures impressing themselves upon the mind and spirit of the prophet.

Remember the story I told earlier about my student and *202*? A similar incident occurred in the same meeting a few moments later. The same man was speaking to a couple about their call to evangelism when he paused and said: "I just saw a picture of a young boy dressed up like General MacArthur. I'll just bet your son's name is Douglas." Sure enough, they have one child, a boy named Douglas. This may strike some of you as a bizarre way for God to communicate to someone. I can only suggest you read your Bible again and take note of how often God does incredibly bizarre and strange things, at least by Western standards. Of course, in the final analysis the issue isn't one of normal versus bizarre but whether the revelatory incident is consistent with Scripture and edifying to those involved.

But how does a prophet know that what he is experiencing or thinking is a revelation of the Holy Spirit rather than from some other source? A related, and perhaps more important, question is: How do the rest of us know? I'll try to answer this critically important question in the next chapter.

Do Prophets Experience Ecstasy?

Much depends on one's definition of ecstasy. It may mean that a person experiences a sense of mental detachment and becomes unaware of surroundings and, in varying degrees, is oblivious to sight or sound. This may or may not entail complete loss of consciousness. Others define ecstasy as something akin to divine seizure in which the Holy Spirit overrides and usurps control of one's faculties of thought and speech.

Paul doesn't teach that ecstasy is a part of the prophetic experience. Several factors support this conclusion.

- Paul assumed the person prophesying was capable of recognizing from some form of signal that someone else had received a revelation and was ready to speak (1 Cor. 14:30). Clearly, then, the prophets were not oblivious to their surroundings.
- The person prophesying was also expected to cease speaking upon recognition that another had received a revelation. ("Let the first keep silent.") The prophet could both speak and keep silent at will. Also, the second prophet didn't burst into speech but somehow indicated to the first, then waited until the first had stopped.
- Paul said that all who prophesied could do so in turn, "one by one" (v. 31), indicating the sensible and voluntary control of their faculties.
- In 1 Corinthians 14:32 Paul said, "The spirits of prophets are subject to prophets." He was referring to the many different manifestations of the one Holy Spirit through the spirit of each individual prophet (see also 14:12, 14-16). This means the Holy Spirit

will never force or compel a prophet to speak, but the Spirit subjects his work to the wisdom of each individual. The Spirit voluntarily submits in this one respect for the sake of order. This isn't a theological declaration that we are in some sense superior to or more powerful than the Holy Spirit. It isn't the nature of the Spirit to incite confusion or to coerce the will; thus, he subordinates his inspiration to the prophet's own timing. This verse also answers the argument of some who might say the Spirit forced them to prophesy and therefore they were unable to restrain themselves or defer to a second message (1 Cor. 14:30). Paul's answer was that the Holy Spirit remains subject to the prophets, never forcing one to speak in a disorderly or chaotic way. The Spirit is neither impetuous nor uncontrollable.

- The case of tongues is in many respects parallel. The tongues-speaker could speak or be silent at will and was expected to follow a prescribed "order of service" in the exercise of the gift (1 Cor. 14:27-28), something out of the question if that person were in any sense mentally disengaged from events in the meeting.

Having ruled out ecstasy does not mean that the prophetic experience lacks an emotional dimension. The reception and communication of divine revelation may well entail spiritual excitement, a sense of urgency, and even an unmistakable sense of the presence of God.

Did Paul Allow Women to Prophesy?

I believe women can and should prophesy. In Peter's speech on the Day of Pentecost he explicitly said that a characteristic of the present church age is the Spirit's impartation of the prophetic gift to both men and women. Look closely at his citation of Joel's promise:

> "And it shall be in the last days," God says, "That I will pour forth of My Spirit on all mankind; and your sons and your *daughters* shall prophesy, and your young men shall see visions, and your old men shall dream dreams; even upon my bondslaves, both men and *women,* I will in those days pour forth of my Spirit, and they shall prophesy."
>
> ACTS 2:17-18, emphasis added

In Acts 21:9 Luke referred to the four daughters of Philip as having the gift of prophecy. And in 1 Corinthians 11:5 Paul gave instructions regarding how women were to pray and prophesy in the church meeting.

In that light, what did Paul mean in 1 Corinthians 14:34 when he wrote, "Let the women keep silent in the churches; for they are not permitted to speak"?

There are more than a dozen competing interpretations, but I will only mention the one I find persuasive. I believe Paul was prohibiting women from participating in the passing of judgment upon or the evaluation of the prophets (14:29). Consider the following evidence.

In the New Testament there are always contextual limitations on the verb *to be silent* (*sigao*). This word never implies total silence on all speech but is contextually restricted. The restriction may be temporal (someone is to be silent *while* someone else is speaking; Acts 12:17; 15:12-13; 1 Cor. 14:30), or topical (the one who is silent does not speak in a certain manner or on a certain topic but can speak in other ways and on other issues; see 1 Cor. 14:28 where the tongues-speaker could certainly participate in singing, praying, reading Scripture, while remaining silent in that realm of concern to the apostle; compare 1 Tim. 2:12 with Titus 2:3-5). Thus Paul would be restricting speech designed to critique prophetic utterances but would not prohibit other forms of verbal participation.

If this interpretation is correct, Paul would be forbidding women to speak in church only in regard to the judgment or evaluation of prophetic utterances. Evidently he believed that this entailed an exercise of authority restricted to men only (see 1 Tim. 2:12-15).

If one should ask why Paul would allow women to prophesy but not evaluate the prophecies of others, the answer is in the nature of prophecy itself. Prophecy, unlike teaching, does not entail the exercise of an authoritative position within the local church. The prophet was but an instrument through whom revelation was reported to the congregation. Grudem explains: "Those who prophesied did not tell the church how to interpret and apply Scripture to life. They did not proclaim the doctrinal and ethical standards by which the church was guided, nor did they exercise governing authority in the church."[3]

But to evaluate or criticize or judge prophetic utterances is another matter. In this activity one could hardly avoid explicit theological and ethical instruction of other believers. If we assume that in 1 Timothy 2 Paul prohibited women from teaching or exercising authority over men (and this, of course, is an extremely controversial passage), it's understandable why he would allow women to prophesy in 1 Corinthians 11:5 but forbid them from judging the prophetic utterances of others (especially men) in 14:34.

This view also explains Paul's appeal to "the Law" (i.e., the Old Testament) in verse 34. The Old Testament does not teach that women are to remain silent at all times in worship (Ex. 15:20-21; 2 Sam. 6:15,19; Ps. 148:12). But it does endorse male headship in the home and in worship, consistent with Paul's teaching here and elsewhere.

Finally, this view helps explain verse 35. If a woman wanted to evade Paul's prohibition, she might say: "OK—I'll obey Paul's directives. But surely no one cares if I just ask a couple of questions." Such apparently "innocent" questioning could then become an opportunity for expressing in a none-too-veiled form the very judgments Paul prohibits. The proper context for this, says Paul, is at home with one's husband.

What Is the Purpose of Most Prophetic Utterances?

Prophetic utterances will edify, exhort, and console (1 Cor. 14:3). When people are suddenly confronted with the inescapable reality that God truly knows their hearts and has heard their prayers and is intimately acquainted with all their ways, they are encouraged to press on and to persevere. I've often spoken with believers who, in spite of what they knew theologically to be true, felt as if God had forgotten them. Their prayers seemed never to be heard, much less answered. Then, often quite without warning, a total stranger gives them a prophetic word that could be known only by God himself, and their faith is bolstered and their spirits consoled.

Prophetic utterances also bring *conviction* as the secrets of the sinner's heart are exposed (1 Cor. 14:24-25). Paul envisioned prophetic utterances *teaching* (1 Cor. 14:31) and even on occasion giving *direction for ministry* (Acts 13:1-3). A young couple from my former church in Oklahoma was considering whether or not God was calling them to leave their lifelong home and move to Kansas City to begin training for the ministry. At a conference in Kansas City one evening they were given a brief, but powerful, word of counsel from a man who had never met them. He said:

> Artie and Jennifer ... Arthur ... and is there a Cheryl? You are friends of Sam's from Oklahoma, and you are wondering about whether or not to move to pursue ministry. Well, pack your bags, because it isn't in Oklahoma.

The significance of this becomes clear when you realize that I had said nothing about an Arthur or Cheryl. Yet these are the names of Artie's father and mother, who live in the small community of Lone Grove, Oklahoma! Perhaps you are wondering, "Why would God reveal the names of a young man's parents in this way?" Again, I believe this was a token to Artie and Jennifer from the Lord himself, alerting them to the fact that the counsel was accurate. There simply is no way this prophetic minister could have obtained such information apart from divine revelation. It is important to point out that this young couple had already decided to move to Kansas City. The prophetic word was a divine confirmation to them that their decision was truly within God's will.

Finally, prophetic utterances may also on occasion contain *warnings* (Acts 21:4, 10-14) or present *opportunities*. Prophetic utterances may even *identify and impart spiritual gifts* (1 Tm. 4:14).

Cautions

Let me conclude with a few words of caution regarding how prophecy is not to be used.

First of all, avoid using prophecy to establish doctrines or practices that lack explicit biblical support. The Bible is the final and all-sufficient treasury of every doctrine or theological truth that God will ever give. Neither should we expect new ethical principles through prophetic ministry. What is right and what is wrong has been finally and forever settled in the written Word of God.

Second, don't appeal to prophecy to set behavioral standards on secondary issues. Be wary of those who claim to know whether or not it is "God's will" that Christians attend movies or drink wine or play pool or engage in other activities not explicitly advocated or prohibited in Scripture.

Third, avoid using prophecy to disclose negative or excessively critical information in public. Remember that, according to 1 Corinthians 14:3, prophecy is designed to encourage, edify, and console people in the church. It is not meant to humiliate or embarrass them.

Fourth, be careful before you yield governmental authority in the church to those who have the gift of prophecy. By all means listen to them! Seek their counsel and insight. But at the same time remember that church leadership is the responsibility of the elders. The New Testament doesn't say, "Be subject to the prophets," but rather, "Be subject to [the] elders" (1 Pet. 5:5; Heb. 13:17). Paul went from city to city to ordain or appoint elders—not prophets (Acts 14:23; 20:17; 1 Tim. 5:17; 1 Pet. 5:2; Titus 1:5). Whereas it's good that some elders/pastors are prophetically gifted, that alone does not qualify them for office. Elders are to be "able to *teach*" (1 Tim. 3:2), not necessarily able to prophesy.

Fifth, be cautious about excessive dependence on prophetic words for making routine, daily decisions in life. However, in certain situations, guidance from a prophetic word is appropriate. The decision facing the young couple from Oklahoma I mentioned earlier is a case in point. Even the apostle Paul occasionally altered his travel and ministry plans based on prophetic revelation (Acts 16 and Gal. 2:1-2).

Typically, though, Paul emphasized the importance of "reckoning" with the circumstances of whatever situation one is facing. Consider the needs of people, the principles of Scripture, and seek the counsel of those who have a track record of wisdom (Phil. 2:25; 1 Cor. 6:5).

Concerning his travel plans, Paul wrote, "And if it is fitting for me to go also, they will go with me" (1 Cor. 16:4). Here Paul planned to make his decision based on a sober evaluation of what was "fitting," or advisable, in view of the circumstances and what he felt would please God. Of course, nothing he said ruled out the possibility that prophetic insight could play a role. In other texts Paul appealed to "knowledge," "discernment," and "spiritual wisdom and understanding" (Phil. 1:9-10a; Col. 1:9) as essential in the decision-making process. Certainly, revelatory insight from the Lord can be crucial in such deliberation, but God does not want us to be paralyzed in its absence.

Finally, resist the pressure to prophesy in the absence of a divine revelation. Prophetically gifted people are under constant pressure to produce on demand. "I need a word from God, and I need it now," is not an uncommon demand made of those in prophetic ministry. At all costs, resist the temptation to speak when God is silent. Some of the most severe denunciations and warnings of judgment are reserved for those who claim to speak for God, but don't (see Ez. 13:1-9; Jer. 23:25-32).

The Gift of Distinguishing of Spirits

This spiritual gift may be the ability to pass discerning judgment on prophetic utterances, thereby standing in relation to the gift of prophecy the way interpretation does to the gift of tongues (1 Cor. 14:29). However, the "others" in 14:29 are probably all other believers, not just a select few with a special gift (see chapter seven, "Who Said God Said?").

I'm inclined to believe that this is the ability to distinguish between works of the Holy Spirit and works of another spirit (demonic) or perhaps even the human spirit. Not all miracles or supernatural displays are produced by the Holy Spirit. Whereas all Christians are responsible to "test the spirits to see whether they be of God" (1 John 4:1), Paul has in mind here a special ability that is fundamentally intuitive or subjective in nature. Given the contextual flow in 1 John, all should test the spirits by evaluating their messages. In particular, do they confess that "Jesus Christ has come in the flesh" (4:2)? This requires no special gifting. But the spiritual gift of distinguishing of spirits is probably a supernaturally enabled sense or feeling concerning the nature and source of the spirit.

Some possible instances where this gift was in operation include:

- Acts 16:16-18, where Paul discerned that the power of a certain slave girl was in fact a demonic spirit.
- Acts 13:8-11, where Paul discerned that Elymas the magician was demonically energized in his attempt to oppose the presentation of the gospel.
- Acts 14:8-10, where again Paul discerned ("saw") that a man had faith to be healed.
- When a person is able to discern whether or not a

problem in someone's life is demonic or merely the consequence of other emotional and psychological factors, or perhaps a complex combination of both.

- When people with this gift are often able to detect or discern the presence of demonic spirits in a room or some such location.
- In Acts 8:20-24, Peter was said to "see" (not physically, but to perceive or sense) that Simon Magus was filled with bitterness and iniquity.
- It would seem that Jesus exercised something along the lines of this gift when he looked at Nathanael and described him as a man "in whom is no guile" (John 1:47). In John 2:25 it is said that Jesus "knew what was in man." Was this a gift of discernment or distinguishing of spirits?

Prophecy is certainly a precious gift of God to his people. But that does not mean it is beyond being abused. Perhaps the greatest disservice we show to those who prophesy is the failure to evaluate what they say in the light of Scripture. I want to address this very point in the next chapter.

SEVEN

Who Said God Said?

The most urgent need for prophetic ministry today isn't the ability to hear God's voice with greater clarity. As important as that is, *the most urgent need is a church that is theologically literate and sufficiently familiar with the Bible that it can effectively judge and evaluate both the source and meaning of dreams, visions, and subjective impressions.*

Those of us who happily embrace the gifts of the Spirit need to honestly face the fact that too often people in prophetic ministry have been less than diligent in their study of the *written* Word of God and therefore less than competent to effectively test and analyze what purports to be the *spoken* Word of God. Some have become so enamored by the sensationalism of spontaneous revelatory words that they have neglected the Scriptures.

A disturbing trend among some in the body of Christ is the failure to be diligent and disciplined in the study of God's Word on the unspoken premise that it's much easier to get a life-changing prophecy than it is to experience the transformation that comes from study of the Scriptures. In one sense they're right. It *is* harder to actively immerse oneself in the rigors of biblical study than it is to passively receive an exciting revelatory word from an anointed prophetic voice. This isn't in any way to minimize, far less to deny, the reality of the latter. But spoken words must never become an excuse for personal sloth when it comes to digging deeply into God's written Word for those treasures that will otherwise remain forever unearthed.

This isn't to suggest that we should pit one against the other:

the written Word of God versus the spoken Word of God. After all, it's in the *written* Word (1 Thess. 5:20 and elsewhere) that Paul told us not to despise the *spoken* Word! But never forget that it is the former which judges and tests the latter.

There are any number of factors why people have grown slack in their duty to judge prophetic words. Some have grown so accustomed to hearing God's voice and having others expect them to hear it or to interpret it for those who claim they've heard it, that they tend not to evaluate. They are only too happy to interpret what they believe is the meaning of the word, but they don't bother to evaluate its origin or validity. They often simply assume or take for granted that what purports to be a prophetic word is wholly from God. They are so excited about prophecy that they are afraid to acknowledge that some so-called words aren't genuine.

Also, it is difficult and unpleasant to challenge someone concerning the validity of a word they have spoken. Confrontation is uncomfortable, and we will often use any excuse to avoid it. After all, we don't want to hurt their feelings or run the risk of shutting them down so that they are afraid ever again to be open to the possibility that God is speaking. This admirable, but misguided, sense of compassion only aggravates the problem.

Others are so concerned about despising prophetic words and quenching the Holy Spirit that they bend over backward not to judge or critically evaluate what is said. Related to this is their fear that if they misjudge a prophetic word they might lose the blessing or benefit that God intended for them to receive through it. They don't want to appear critical, far less skeptical, of what may well be the voice of heaven.

Someone once justified to me their reluctance to critically evaluate a prophetic word by saying, "I want to be able to respond as Mary, the mother of Jesus did when Gabriel brought news of her impending virginal conception: 'Be it done unto me according to thy word.'" This person mistakenly believed that to respond with anything other than unquestioning faith and submission to the word might disqualify them from reaping the fruit that it was designed to produce in their lives. I understand their zeal. To a degree I actually find it commendable. But it can also be extremely dangerous. Paul's exhortation to judge all prophetic words means that it is *not* lack of faith if you first evaluate what is said.

Then there is the additional factor that I call *prophetic awe*. By that I mean the awe, indeed the virtual reverence, which some people have for those who are especially gifted in prophetic ministry. Some are so much in awe of certain prophets that the moment the prophets open their mouths the people put their brains in neutral, cast discernment to the wind, and never think about opening the Bible to see whether or not what the prophets are saying is really true. The result is that all sorts of flaky, unbiblical ideas get passed off as divine revelation. Worse still, people end up getting hurt, used, and manipulated, and prophecy itself ends up being mocked by those outside the church and minimized by those inside. This must stop. Let me simply remind you that the apostle Paul was in no way offended or put off by the Bereans who "examined the Scriptures" to determine whether or not what he said was true (Acts 17:10-11).

Prophecy is too precious and too important for the church to let this sort of abuse continue any longer. Some who believe in the gift of prophecy and zealously desire to excel in its exercise have overreacted to the skepticism and cynicism of those Christians who believe that prophecy died with the apostle John. This overreaction has resulted in an equally dangerous response: gullibility and empty-headed acceptance of any so-called word that is uttered. Both of these responses to prophecy will ultimately destroy its effectiveness in the church.

The Biblical Mandate

Look at Paul's counsel in 1 Thessalonians 5:19-22. Many read this as a general exhortation concerning our response to good and evil. But this entire passage is specifically describing the responsibility of the entire church to judge prophetic utterances:

> Do not quench the Spirit (v. 19); do not despise prophetic utterances (v. 20). But examine everything carefully; hold fast to that which is good (v. 21); abstain from every form of evil (v. 22).

Observe the parallel between verse 19 and verse 20. Paul's exhortation in verse 19 not to quench the Spirit has to do with our response to prophecy (v. 20). It may well have application to the exercise of other spiritual gifts in the church, but its first and primary reference is to the gift of prophecy. The Spirit's activity of imparting revelatory insight into the will and ways of God is compared with a fire that we must not douse with the water of skepticism, religiosity, or fear.

Perhaps most important of all is the word *but* with which verse 21 opens. Clearly Paul is setting up a contrast. *Rather than* quenching the Holy Spirit by despising prophetic utterances, examine everything. "Everything" or "all things" in verse 21 refesr to the prophetic utterances in verse 20.

This leads to the conclusion that the "good," to which we are to hold fast (v. 21), and the "evil," from which we are to abstain or which we are to avoid (v. 22), are also references to prophetic utterances (v. 20). Most have appealed to verses 21-22 as a general exhortation to help us in our response to good and evil in the world. But when looked at in the light of the overall context, we see that the "good" are those prophetic utterances that truly come from God and encourage, edify, and console, whereas the "evil" refers to what alleges to be revelation from God but in fact is not, having been shown to be inconsistent with Scripture.

The fact that Paul felt compelled to write this is itself remarkably instructive. For one thing, it tells us that not everyone in the early church was completely happy about the gift of prophecy. Some were clearly disenchanted with its use in the church and were actually taking steps to suppress its exercise. This is remarkable for no other reason than that it was happening in the church at Thessalonica, one of the most godly and mature early congregations (see Paul's praise of them in 1 Thess. 1:1-10).

Why were some in Thessalonica "despising" (NASB) or treating "with contempt" (NIV) prophetic words? Probably for the same reason that people do so today! Undoubtedly the prophetic gift had been abused in Thessalonica, prompting some to call for its elimination altogether. Some may have abused the gift by using it to control other people's lives or to increase their sphere of influence and power in the church.

Perhaps it had been overused. We know that in Corinth those with the prophetic gift tended to dominate the public meetings of the church, forcing Paul to lay down strict guidelines for prophecy in group settings (1 Cor. 14:29-36). I suspect that prophetic words had not been properly judged. Problems had arisen from people gullibly and naively accepting every word as being "from God." No doubt there were some who thought prophecy was weird and were embarrassed by its use in the congregation.

Some probably claimed to be special to God, uniquely favored, or more spiritual and more mature simply because they had this gift. Those without the gift would be understandably fed up with this kind of elitism and perhaps responded by insisting that such activity be strictly controlled and even suppressed. It may well be that some were disillusioned with words that didn't seem to have come true and in their woundedness overreacted to the mere presence of this gift in the church. It isn't uncommon for people to mistakenly assume that a prophecy is an infallible guarantee when in reality a prophecy more often takes the form of merely an invitation or exhortation. We know that the people in Thessalonica were a bit skittish about alleged prophetic words, as the scenario described in 2 Thessalonians 2:1-2 makes clear.

Don't miss the force of what Paul was saying. Simply put, it doesn't matter how badly people may have abused this gift. It is a *sin* to despise prophecy. This is a divine command. Don't treat prophecy with contempt; don't treat it as if it were unimportant; don't trivialize it. In other words, there is a real, live baby in that murky, distasteful bath water. So be careful that when you throw out the latter you don't dispense with the former!

This exhortation also means that if you *do* despise prophecy, if you seek to exclude it from your church life, if you flippantly disregard it, you have "quenched the Holy Spirit," you have put out his fire! That in itself is incredibly revealing about how the Holy Spirit ministers through us. He will rarely, if ever, force himself in a manifestation or display of a gift or any other supernatural or natural expression. The Spirit willingly subjects himself to the will and timing of the believer (see 1 Cor. 14:32). The Holy Spirit does not act upon or through us as if we were puppets. The sovereign Spirit happily subjects himself to our decision concerning when and how we deliver prophetic words. Not only that, but it also means that you can sinfully put out the Spirit's fire that is burning in someone else's heart! This is dangerous ground on which to tread!

So what is the alternative to not quenching the Holy Spirit when he speaks prophetically through someone? It isn't "anything goes." Rather, we are to test, judge, or examine every word. Paul didn't correct abuse by commanding disuse (as is the practice of many non-charismatics today). We are neither to gullibly believe every word that is spoken nor cynically reject all. Paul's remedy for sinful despising wasn't unqualified openness. His remedy was biblically informed discernment.

Weighing a Word

What, then, is our responsibility when prophecies are given? Quite simply, we are to test, to examine, to evaluate, to assess, to weigh, to judge these "utterances" (NASB).[1] Paul's exhortation is three-fold: examine everything, hold fast to that which is good, abstain from every form of evil. Let's look at practical ways that we do these things.

Examine Everything
He first commanded them to "examine everything." By "everything" Paul didn't mean everything in general, but, in light of the context, he meant "all prophetic utterances." But how do we examine or test them? Here are a few suggestions.

The early church was to evaluate prophecies in the light of the apostolic traditions (2 Thess. 2:15) bequeathed them by Paul. The reference to what they were "taught ... by word of mouth" obviously alludes to the oral instruction received from Paul during his stay in Thessalonica. The "letter" Paul mentioned is likely a reference either to 1 Thessalonians or 2 Thessalonians.

For us today, all prophetic words must be in absolute conformity with Scripture. In the wilderness, Jesus tested Satan's words against what the rest of Scripture said and exposed how he was misapplying texts (see Matt. 4).

We also measure a prophetic word by its tendency to edify (1 Cor. 14:3). We must always ask: Does it build up and strengthen, or does it tear down and create disunity and fear and doubt and self-contempt? Does the word have a tendency to exhort and encourage (1 Cor. 14:3)? Does the word have a tendency to console (1 Cor. 14:3), or does it lead to despair? If the word is predictive, find out whether or not the event came to pass as prophesied.

We must also apply the test of love (1 Cor. 13), by which all charismatic gifts are to be measured and subordinated. Paul didn't appear to care much for any gift of the Spirit if it violated the dictates of love. The test of community is also important. Wisdom demands that we always present the word to others who have skill and experience in evaluating prophetic revelation.

Finally, there is the test of personal experience. When Paul was given a word about the danger that awaited him in Jerusalem (Acts 21:3-4 and 21:10-14), he evaluated and then responded in the light of what God had already told and shown him (20:22-23). In effect, Paul said: "Yes, we all got the same revelation and interpretation that suffering awaits me in Jerusalem, but we differ on its application."

Hold Fast to the Good

Paul's second exhortation is to "hold fast to that which is good." Once you have determined that the word is *good*, that it is biblical and meets all other criteria and is therefore most probably from God, believe it, obey it, preserve it.

Abstain From Every Form of Evil

Paul's third exhortation was to "abstain from every form of evil." The word "abstain" (NASB) or "avoid" (NIV) is also found in 1 Thessalonians 4:3 ("abstain from sexual immorality") and 1 Timothy 4:3 ("abstaining from foods"). The word translated "form" or "kind" is used only here in Paul's writings. Hence, "Shun every kind of prophetic utterance that is evil," that doesn't conform to Scripture, that doesn't build up and encourage and exhort and console.

Practical Implications

This leads to several important conclusions. First, this means that in a manner of speaking, prophets can speak both good and evil words. But remember, evil can come in various shades of black! There is evil that simply means it isn't good or effective in doing what Scripture says prophecy should do. In this case, evil means "ineffective" or "unfruitful." Or evil may mean "contrary to Scripture." It doesn't necessarily mean "hateful, mean, sinister, wicked, or motivated by a desire to inflict harm on you." It simply means a word that fails to accomplish what true prophetic words are designed by God to accomplish.

Second, this means that we must not assume that every idea or image or word that pops into our heads (or the head of a recognized prophet) is a revelation from God.

Third, it means there is a vast difference between prophesying falsely and being a false prophet. All of us have at one time or another, some more, some less, prophesied falsely. We have spoken words we thought were from God which, in fact, were not. But that doesn't make us false prophets. It just makes us human! False prophets are indeed spoken of in the New Testament, but they were not Christians who made errors in prophetic words. False prophets were non-Christian enemies of the gospel (Matt. 7:15-23; 24:10-11, 24; 2 Pet. 2:1-3; 1 John 4:1-6).

Passing Judgment (1 Cor. 14:29)[2]

The other text relevant to judging prophetic words is found in 1 Corinthians 14:29. There Paul wrote: "And let two or three prophets speak, *and let the others pass judgment.*"

Does Paul's statement that we are to "let two or three prophets speak" in a meeting imply that *more* would be in violation of God's Word? If so, his point would be to limit the number to three lest those with this gift dominate the meeting. There is similar instruction in verse 27 concerning those who speak in tongues. On the other hand, verses 24 and 31 seem to suggest that many might prophesy in a meeting. In that case, there should be no more than three at a time before the others weigh carefully what is said. In other words, verse 29 may be designed to restrict how many may speak *in sequence* but not the total number of prophecies given in any one service.

The "others" who are to pass judgment are probably the others in the congregation as a whole, that is to say, all other believers present. First Thessalonians 5:20-21, which calls for the evaluation of prophetic utterances, is directed to the entire church, not a specially gifted group.[3]

What is the nature of this judgment to be passed? It isn't the determination of whether the utterance is of the Spirit or of the devil, but whether the utterance is compatible with what the Spirit has already said (in Scripture, in the apostolic tradition, etc.). If New Testament congregational prophecy is occasionally a mixture of divine revelation and human interpretation and application (Acts 21:4-6; 21:10-14, 27-35), it's essential that the church evaluate and analyze what is said, rejecting what is wrong and accepting what is right (1 Thess. 5:19-22; see also 1 John 4:1-6). Only on the assumption that some of what the prophets say is their own contribution, and therefore possibly erroneous or misleading, could Paul command that their utterances be evaluated. Says Grudem:

> As a prophet was speaking, each member of the congregation would listen carefully, evaluating the prophecy in the light of the Scripture and the authoritative teaching which he or she already knew to be true. Soon there would be an opportunity to speak in the response, with the wise and mature no doubt making the most contribution. But no member of the body would have needed to feel useless, for every member at least silently would weigh and evaluate what was said.[4]

The take-away from this chapter is simple. Anytime you are the recipient of a prophetic word, open your Bible and carefully assess what was said. To do so isn't a sign of unbelief or cynicism or pride, far less suspicion of the person who spoke it. It's your Christian obligation. My hope is that each of us will determine in our hearts neither to be skeptics who end up putting out the Spirit's fire nor fools who gullibly believe everything we are told.

Answering Arguments Against Prophecy for Today

I've referred on several occasions to my contribution to the book *Are Miraculous Gifts for Today? Four Views*. Much of the authors' interaction in that book centered around this question: How would we today respond if God spoke prophetically to us in the same way he did to Christians in the first century?

Richard Gaffin, who defended the cessationist view, objected to the possibility of postcanonical revelation on grounds that we would be bound to attend and submit to it *no less than to Scripture*. But the problem of Christians being obligated to submit to the authority of "words" other than Scripture words is one the cessationist himself must face. Remember that Paul instructed the Thessalonian Christians to place great value upon prophetic utterances. They were "bound to attend and submit to" (literally, "hold fast"; 1 Thess. 5:21) the prophetic words they received, just as much as they were "bound to attend and submit to" the Scripture in which this very instruction is found. Evidently Paul didn't fear that their response to the spoken, prophetic word would undermine the ultimate authority or sufficiency of the written revelation (Scripture) that he was in the process of sending them. The point is this: noncanonical revelation was not inconsistent with the authority of Scripture *then*, nor need it be *now*. This is especially true if, as I have argued, contemporary prophecy is presumed to yield words that are occasionally a mix of fallible and infallible.

Someone might ask, "But how should we in the twenty-first century, in a closed-canonical world, respond to non-canonical revelation?" The answer is, "In the same way Christians, such as the Thessalonians, responded to it in their first-century, open-canonical world, namely, by *evaluating it in light of Scripture*" (which was emerging, and therefore partial, for them but is complete for us). Such revelation would carry for us today the same authority it carried then for them. Furthermore, we're in a much better position today than the early church, for we have the final form of the canon by which to evaluate claims to prophetic revelation. If they were capable of assessing prophetic revelation then (and Paul believed they were; witness his instruction in 1 Thessalonians 5 and 1 Corinthians 14 to do precisely that), how much more are we today!

If noncanonical revelation was not a threat to the ultimate authority of Scripture in Scripture's emerging form, neither should it pose a threat to Scripture in its final form. The first-century Christians were obligated to believe and obey Scripture in the open-canonical period, simultaneous with and in the presence of non-canonical prophetic revelation. There is no reason to think non-canonical revelation in the closed-canonical period of church history would present any more of a problem.

In a related vein, Gaffin argued that contemporary prophecy cannot, in fact, be evaluated by Scripture because of the prophecy's purported specificity. But this again is no more a problem for us today than it would have been for Christians in the first century. Didn't they evaluate prophetic revelation in spite of its specificity and individuality? If they were obedient to Paul's instruction, they certainly did (1 Cor. 14:29; 1 Thess. 5:21-22). We can do the same. Remember, we are actually better equipped to assess prophecies than they were because we hold in hand the final form of canonical revelation by which we can make such judgments.

Gaffin also insisted that to admit the possibility of revelation beyond Scripture necessarily implies a certain insufficiency in Scripture that needs to be compensated for. But one must ask, "For what is Scripture sufficient?" Certainly it is sufficient to provide us with those theological truths and principles essential for a life of godliness. Yet Gaffin conceded that God reveals himself to individuals in a variety of personal, highly intimate ways. But there would be no need for him to do this if Scripture were as exhaustively sufficient as Gaffin elsewhere insists. That God should find it important and helpful to reveal himself to his children in personal and intimate ways bears witness to the fact that the sufficiency of the Bible is not meant to suggest that we need no longer hear from our heavenly Father or receive particular guidance in areas on which the Bible is silent.

Scripture never claims to supply us with all possible information necessary to make every conceivable decision. Scripture may tell us to preach the gospel to all people, but it does not tell a new missionary in 2002, that God desires his service in Albania rather than Australia. The potential for God's speaking beyond Scripture, whether for guidance, exhortation, encouragement, or conviction of sin poses no threat to the sufficiency that Scripture claims for itself.

EIGHT

What Is the Gift of Tongues?

"I thank God I speak in tongues more than you all."

You might think these are the words of an obscure medieval mystic or perhaps a flamboyant charismatic making a guest appearance on TBN's *Praise the Lord* broadcast. To the surprise of many, they are in fact the words of Paul of Tarsus, apostle of Jesus Christ, theological genius, and author of Scripture (1 Cor. 14:18). Evidently, Paul's religious life was regularly given to praying, singing, and praising in tongues, and he was not in the least bit hesitant or embarrassed to say so. Indeed, he was profoundly grateful to God that he had received this gift. If nothing else, this ought to give us pause before we so quickly dismiss tongues as the habit of overly emotional and ill-informed fanatics. The gift of tongues is simply the Spirit-energized ability to pray, worship, give thanks, or speak in a language other than your own or one you might have learned in school.

The gift of tongues was perhaps the single most divisive and controversial issue in twentieth-century Christianity. There have been heated squabbles in the church over such things as the role of women, the time of the rapture, water baptism, the inerrancy of Scripture, and the millennium, but nothing can compare with the hostility and name-calling provoked by the debate over the nature and validity of contemporary tongues-speech. People are rarely neutral about this spiritual gift.

I was raised in a tradition that viewed speaking in tongues as barely a notch above snake-handling. Ignorant and undignified people spoke in tongues, probably with eyes rolled back in their sockets while on the verge of something akin to an epileptic seizure—or so I was led to believe. People who could read and write and hoped to make their mark in the world, on the other hand, wouldn't be caught dead muttering that sort of gibberish or associating with those who did. Or so I was led to believe.

I know what it's like to feel revulsion toward speaking in tongues. For many years I mocked those who claimed to experience this phenomenon. I know what it's like to feel embarrassed by a sudden, uninterpreted outburst that shatters the solemnity of a worship service and disrupts the sense of holy awe and reverence. But I urge you not to let the discomfort caused by an unseemly incident forever harden you against the possibility that this might well be a gift of God. We must never forget that the gift of tongues was God's idea, not man's. He gave this gift to the church no less than the gifts of teaching, mercy, exhortation, and evangelism. Let's resolve from the outset not to spurn or ridicule something precious in God's sight, graciously bestowed by a loving heavenly Father who gives only good gifts to his children.

It's also important that we keep our sense of perspective. Tongues is neither God's greatest gift to his most highly favored children nor is it the devil's most sinister tool of deceit. Tongues is just like any other gift of the Spirit. It is not a sign of God's special love. It is not a sign of heightened maturity in Christ. It is not a sign of superior zeal or commitment. It is not a sign that one has more of the Holy Spirit than others. In fact, *tongues is not a sign of anything*. It is merely one among many of what the apostle Paul calls "manifestations of the Spirit" (1 Cor. 12:7) given to believers for the common good of the church.

Contrary to the caricatures that many have of the gift of tongues, most will testify how it has served to enhance and deepen their relationship with the Lord Jesus (which is precisely what prayer and praise are supposed to do!). Believe it or not, they can still tie their shoelaces, balance a checkbook, drive a car, hold down a job, and they rarely ever drool! I don't mean to be sarcastic, but this gift of the Spirit has a terrible public image. For people to reveal they speak in tongues is to risk being perceived as mindless, spiritually flabby fanatics who periodically mumble while in a convulsive or hypnotic trance. I would simply encourage you to search the Scriptures, seek the face of God, and continue reading as I attempt to provide a biblical foundation for the understanding and exercise of this gift of the Spirit.

I encourage you to read what follows with an open Bible. If what I say doesn't measure up to the written Word of God, dump it. Experience is only as good as it reflects the teaching of Holy Scripture. Frankly, I'm a bit fed up with the charge that people who believe in the gifts of the Holy Spirit are either too lazy to think or refuse to do so from fear that the Bible might contradict their experience. I'm not in the least bit afraid of the Bible.

Were Tongues Evangelistic?

There is no evidence that tongues-speech was designed to evangelize unbelievers. That isn't to say God couldn't use it to save souls, or even as a form of pre-evangelism, but that's not its primary purpose. When people spoke in tongues they declared "the mighty deeds of God" (Acts 2:11; observe the same phrase in Acts 10:46 and 19:17). The people don't hear an evangelistic message but rather worship. It is only Peter's preaching that brought salvation. Here, as elsewhere, we see that the primary purpose of tongues-speech is address to God, whether it be praise or prayer (1 Cor. 14:2, 14). And when the household of Cornelius spoke in tongues, far from questioning the sanity or stability of these believing Gentiles, Peter concluded that they were saved and thus eligible to be baptized in water no less than had they been Jews who accepted Jesus (v. 47).

In the Book of Acts, some, but not all, who received Christ as Savior spoke in tongues immediately upon their conversion. There are several instances of conversion in Acts where no mention is made of speaking in tongues.[1] This doesn't prove they didn't. But neither should one conclude that they did.

Only in Acts 2 are tongues explicitly said to be human languages not previously learned by the speaker (more on this below). Nowhere in Acts did speaking in tongues function as an evangelistic tool, nor do we ever find an apostolic exhortation that it be used for that purpose. In the three explicit references to tongues in Acts, only once (Acts 2) are unbelievers present. Some cessationists argue that tongues were primarily an evangelistic sign-gift for unbelieving Jews. That view is greatly weakened by that fact that only *believers* were present at two of the three occurrences of tongues in Acts. I'll return to this point when we come to 1 Corinthians 14.

Tongues-Speech in 1 Corinthians

There are a number of disputed passages in Paul's letters that some believe refer to tongues, but our focus will be on several principles found in 1 Corinthians 12-14.

Before turning there, however, I need to make one comment. Some point out that tongues-speech is explicitly mentioned in no New Testament epistle aside from 1 Corinthians (unless, of course, Eph. 6:18 and Rom. 8:26-27 refer to tongues). They then conclude that the gift of tongues was either infrequently exercised or "on its way out," so to speak. But this is an argument from silence that, if consistently applied to Scripture, results in distorted interpretations. For example, the Lord's Supper is explicitly mentioned only in 1 Corinthians. But surely no one would conclude that it was for this reason infrequently observed or obsolete! Furthermore, the silence of other New Testament epistles can just as easily (and more sensibly) be explained by the fact that, unlike in Corinth, tongues was not a problem in the other churches to whom Paul wrote and ministered. There would be no need for him to address an issue if it were not posing a threat to the church.

It's unfortunate that the image many have of speaking in tongues is shaped by their familiarity with one, somewhat negative, statement by Paul in 1 Corinthians 13:1: "If I speak with the tongues of men and of angels, but do not have love, I have become a noisy gong or a clanging cymbal." But let's not forget that what Paul says here was due to the *abuse* of this spiritual gift in Corinth. If Paul were writing to a church in which tongues was properly employed, perhaps his words would have been phrased something like this: "If I speak with the tongues of men and of angels and do so with love and compassion for my fellow man, the sound is like that of a glorious symphony that pleases the ear."

The problem in Corinth was not that they spoke in tongues, but that those who did so thought themselves spiritually superior or more highly favored than those who didn't. To make matters worse, they were using the gift in the public gathering of the church without accompanying interpretation. Paul addressed the former problem in chapters twelve to thirteen and took up the latter in chapter fourteen.

The Nature of Tongues

The primary thing that concerned Paul in 1 Corinthians 14 was the edification of believers in the church (1 Cor. 14:3-6, 12, 17, 19, 26). But others can be built up and fortified in their faith only if they understand what is being said. This is why he insisted repeatedly that tongues in the assembly must be interpreted.

Don't misunderstand Paul's contrasts. Prophecy is superior to uninterpreted tongues *only* because, being intelligible, it edifies others. When tongues are interpreted they become a *functional equivalent* of prophecy (1 Cor. 14:5). Uninterpreted tongues are unintelligible and therefore can't edify others and for that reason alone are regarded as inferior to prophecy. Interpreted tongues are intelligible and do edify as a result. For this reason, don't forbid them (v. 39).

Paul's concern was the *relative* importance of prophecy and tongues. He was not suggesting that prophecy is the absolutely most important gift or that the gift of tongues is the absolutely least important one. He was only saying that *uninterpreted* tongues are less valuable than prophecy in the gathered assembly How tongues or prophecy might compare with apostleship or teaching or administration or any other gift wasn't in Paul's mind at this point.

Don't miss the fact that Paul's command in 12:31 and 14:1, 39, as well as his statement in 14:12, all indicate that we are to *desire* and *seek* spiritual gifts! Far from being a sign of immaturity or an illegal hankering after sensational phenomena (as some cessationists contend), *seeking spiritual gifts is a moral and biblical obligation for all Christians.*

Paul's statement in 1 Corinthians 14:2 is crucial for understanding tongues. Four things are said. First, tongues-speech is directed or addressed to God, not to men. Tongues, whether spoken or sung, are fundamentally worship and intercession! Even when interpreted in a public gathering, tongues-speech is God-oriented.

Second, no one in the church understands tongues. Why? Because it is uninterpreted. This is the reason for the relative "inferiority" of tongues to prophecy. The importance of this statement for determining if tongues are always human languages will become evident in a moment.

Third, Paul said that "in" or "by" his spirit (*Holy* Spirit?) he speaks mysteries. But whose or what spirit did Paul have in mind? In 1 Corinthians 12:7-11 we are told that "gifts" are manifestations of the Holy Spirit. Perhaps Paul intended to blend the two, the idea being that it is the *Holy* Spirit through *my human* spirit whereby the gift is exercised.

Fourth, and more important still, what is meant by "mysteries"? This may refer to truths relating to our salvation in Christ that were not previously revealed during the era of the Old Testament but now have been made known by an act of revelation. More likely Paul was referring to anything that lies outside the understanding of both the speaker and the hearer. In other words, he speaks mysteries in the sense that no one understands. Tongues-speech, when uninterpreted, is simply a mystery to everyone.

Prophecy, on the other hand, does what uninterpreted tongues can't do, and is for that reason to be preferred in the public gathering of the church. Prophecy edifies and exhorts and consoles (1 Cor. 14:3).

Is Self-Edification OK?

Some argue that Paul was being sarcastic in verse 4, intending to censure or rebuke as selfish anyone who desires to be edified by the use of this gift. But the edifying of oneself is not a bad thing. It simply isn't the primary point of the kind of public meeting Paul had in view. We study the Bible to edify ourselves. We pray to edify ourselves. We listen to sermons to edify ourselves. Countless Christian activities are an effective means of self-edification. I hope that your motivation in reading this book is to edify yourself by increasing your biblical understanding of spiritual gifts! If there are any lingering doubts, Jude 20 commands us to edify ourselves by praying in the Spirit!

Every gift of the Spirit in some way or degree, either directly or indirectly, edifies its user. This is not evil unless self-edification becomes an end in itself. If your spiritual gift serves to increase your maturity, heighten your sensitivity, expand your understanding, and intensify your zeal, all the better for the body of Christ! In this way self-edification is simply an intermediate step to the growth of others in the church. Why would anyone object to that? I'm sure Paul wouldn't.

Also, if self-edification from tongues-speech were wrong, Paul would not have encouraged its use in verse 5a. And uninterpreted tongues *were* what Paul had in mind, for he contrasted them with prophecy, insisting that the latter is better suited to edify others (unless, of course, the tongues-speech is interpreted, v. 5b).

Some may wonder how mysteries that are not understood even by the speaker can edify. The answer lies in verses 14-15. As Gordon Fee pointed out,

> Contrary to the opinion of many, spiritual edification can take place in ways other than through the cortex of the brain. Paul believed in an immediate communing with God by means of the S/spirit that sometimes bypassed the mind; and in verses 14-15 he argues that for his own

edification he will have both. But *in church* he will have only what can also communicate to other believers through their minds.[2]

Is Ecstasy a Part of the Gift of Tongues?

Is tongues-speech an ecstatic experience? It's important to remember that the New Testament never uses the term *ecstasy* to describe speaking in tongues. It is found in some English translations but is not in the Greek text. Many define *ecstatic* as a mental or emotional state in which the person is more or less oblivious to the external world. The individual is perceived as losing self-control, perhaps lapsing into a frenzied condition in which self-consciousness and the power for rational thinking are eclipsed.

There is no indication anywhere in the Bible that people who speak in tongues lose self-control or become unaware of their surroundings. Paul insists that the one speaking in tongues can start and stop at will (1 Cor. 14:15-19; 14:27-28; 14:40; compare with 14:32). There is a vast difference between an experience being ecstatic and it being emotional. Tongues are often a highly emotional and exhilarating experience, bringing peace, joy, etc., but that does not mean they are ecstatic.

Can Everyone Speak in Tongues?

Contrary to some distortions, Paul nowhere denigrated the gift of tongues. He wished all Christians spoke in tongues (1 Cor. 14:5). He applauded the capacity of tongues to edify the believer (v. 4). He thanked God for tongues in his own prayer life

(vv. 18-19) and explicitly warned against any temptation to forbid the exercise of this precious gift (v. 39)!

But we're still left with the most controversial issue relating to tongues-speech: Does Paul's statement in verse 5 mean that *all* Christians should or will speak in tongues?

Those who say no point to several important facts. First, they point to 1 Corinthians 7:7 where Paul uses language identical to what is found in 14:5: *"I wish* that all men were even as I myself am [referring to his celibacy]." No one will argue that Paul intended for all Christians to be celibate as he was. Surely, then, we should not expect all to speak in tongues either. Second, according to 1 Corinthians 12:7-11, tongues, like the other gifts mentioned, is bestowed to individuals as the Holy Spirit wills. If Paul meant that all were to experience this gift, why did he employ the terminology of "to one is given ... and to another ... and to another ..."

The final argument for this view is 1 Corinthians 12:28-30 where Paul quite explicitly stated that "all do not speak with tongues" any more than all are apostles or all are teachers or all have gifts of healings and so on.

But the debate doesn't end there. Those answering yes to our question begin by pointing out that 1 Corinthians 7:7 isn't the only place where Paul uses the "I want" or "I wish" terminology. One must also address 1 Corinthians 10:1; 11:3; and 12:1, texts in which what the apostle wants applies to all believers. Furthermore, in 1 Corinthians 7 Paul said explicitly why his wish for universal celibacy cannot and should not be fulfilled. But in 1 Corinthians 14 no such contextual clues are found that suggest Paul's wish for all to speak in tongues cannot be fulfilled.

The question may also be asked, "Why would God withhold from any of his children a gift that enables them to pray and to praise him so effectively, a gift which also functions to edify them in their faith?" And does not 1 Corinthians 14:23 at least imply that the potential exists for all to speak in tongues?

Some people believe the answer lies in looking at the setting in which tongues are exercised. Perhaps 1 Corinthians 12:7-11 and 12:28-30 refer to the gift in *public ministry*, whereas 1 Corinthians 14 is describing the gift in *private devotion*. In 1 Corinthians 12:28 Paul specifically said he was describing what happens "in the church" or "in the assembly" (compare with 11:18; 14:19, 23, 28, 33, 35). Not everyone is gifted by the Spirit to speak in tongues during the corporate gathering of the church. But the potential does exist for every believer to pray in tongues in private. These are not two different gifts, however, but two different contexts in which the one gift might be employed. A person who ministers to the entire church in tongues is someone who already uses tongues in his or her prayer life.

Jack Hayford argues in much the same way, using different terms. He suggests that the *gift* of tongues is (1) limited in distribution (1 Cor. 12:11, 30), and (2) its public exercise is to be closely governed (1 Cor. 14:27-28); while the *grace* of tongues is so broadly available that Paul wished that all enjoyed its blessing (1 Cor. 14:5a), which includes (1) distinctive communication with God (1 Cor. 14:2); (2) edifying of the believer's private life (1 Cor. 14:4); and (3) worship and thanksgiving with beauty and propriety (1 Cor. 14:15-17).[3]

The difference between these operations of the Holy Spirit is that *not every* Christian has reason to expect he or she will necessarily exercise the public *gift*, while *any* Christian may expect and welcome the private *grace* of spiritual language in his or her personal time of prayer fellowship *with* God (1 Cor. 14:2), praiseful worship *before* God (1 Cor. 14:15-17), and intercessory prayer *to* God (Rom. 8:26-27).

Paul's point at the end of 1 Corinthians 12 is that not every believer will contribute to the body in precisely the same way. Not everyone will minister a prophetic word, not everyone will teach, and so on. But whether or not everyone might pray privately in tongues is another matter, not in Paul's purview until chapter 14.

Consider what Paul said about prophecy. "All are not prophets, are they?" (1 Cor. 12:29). No, of course not. But Paul is quick to say that the potential exists for all to prophesy (14:1, 31). Why could not the same be true for tongues? Couldn't Paul have been saying, whereas all do not speak in tongues as an expression of corporate, public ministry, it is possible that all may speak in tongues as an expression of private praise and prayer? Just as Paul's rhetorical question in 12:29 is not designed to rule out the possibility that all may utter a prophetic word, so also his rhetorical question in 12:30 is not designed to exclude anyone from exercising tongues in their private devotional experience.

To be honest, I'm not sure how to answer this question. I must confess it seems unlikely that God would withhold the gift of tongues from one of his children if they passionately and sincerely desire it. My suspicion is that, all things being equal, if you deeply desire this gift it is probably because the Holy Spirit has stirred your heart to seek for it. And he has stirred your heart to seek for it because it is his will to bestow it. So, if you long for the gift of tongues, persevere in your prayers. My sense (with no guarantee) is that God will answer you in his time with a satisfying yes.

Paul's Prayer Life

In describing his own gift of speaking in tongues, Paul wrote, "My spirit prays" (1 Cor. 14:14). This may be a reference to the Holy Spirit, or perhaps his own human spirit, or even a co-working of the two, which in effect constitutes the essence of a spiritual gift. (A spiritual gift is when the Holy Spirit energizes and enables my spirit to do what otherwise I couldn't do.) The important point, however, is that when Paul prays in tongues his mind is "unfruitful." By this he means either, "I don't understand what I am saying," or, "Other people don't understand what I'm saying." The former is more likely.

This is crucial. Many insist that if one's mind is unfruitful, that is to say, if one's mind is not engaged in such a way that the believer can rationally and cognitively grasp what is occurring, the experience, whatever its nature may be, is useless. The apostle Paul strongly disagreed. Since Paul asserted that his mind was unfruitful when he prayed in tongues, many would think his next step would be to repudiate the use of tongues altogether. After all, what possible benefit can there be in a spiritual experience that one's mind can't comprehend? At the very least one would expect Paul to say something to minimize its importance so as to render it trite, at least in comparison with other gifts. But he does no such thing.

Look closely at Paul's conclusion. He even introduced his conclusion by asking the question, in view of what has just been said in verse 14, "What is the outcome then?" (v. 15a). In other words, what am I to do? His answer may come as a shock to you.

He was determined to do both! "I shall pray with the spirit [i.e., I will pray in tongues], and I will pray with the mind [i.e., I will pray in Greek so that others who speak and understand Greek can profit from what I say]." Clearly, Paul believed that a spiritual experience that was beyond the grasp of his mind was yet profoundly profitable. *Paul believed that it wasn't absolutely necessary for an experience to be rationally cognitive for it to be spiritually beneficial and glorifying to God.*

This isn't in any way to denigrate or impugn the crucial importance of one's mind in the Christian life. In Romans 12:1 Paul commanded that we experience renewal in our minds. All I'm saying—what I believe *Paul* is saying—is that praying in tongues is eminently beneficial and glorifying to God even though it is trans-rational in nature.

Furthermore, since Paul was determined to pray with the spirit (i.e., pray in uninterpreted tongues), where and when would he do it? Since he ruled out doing it in the public meeting, he must have been referring to his private, devotional prayer life. To "sing in or with the spirit" is to sing in tongues, a more melodious, musical form of tongues-speech, a practice which also, no doubt, characterized Paul's private prayer experience.

The reference (vv. 16-17) to the "ungifted" (NASB) or "those who do not understand" (NIV) probably points to anyone who does not have the gift of interpretation. It is obviously another Christian, for such a person is capable of being edified and is expected to say amen. Paul also clearly asserted that tongues-speech, among other things, blesses and gives thanks and is thus a form of prayer and praise. However, unless such prayer or praise is understood by others present, God may enjoy it but no one else does.

It is hard to imagine Paul saying anything more explosive than what we now read in verses 18-19. Clearly, Paul's devotional life was characterized by praying and singing and praising in tongues, and he was profoundly grateful to God for this gift. His point in verse 19 is simple: the crucial issue is not whether one speaks in tongues, but what is appropriate in the public assembly of the church.

Paul had said that tongues-speech in the public gathering of the church is prohibited without an interpretation. Since the purpose of church meetings is the edification of other believers, Paul preferred to speak in a language all could understand. Consequently, he rarely spoke in tongues in a public setting. Now note well: if Paul spoke in tongues more frequently and fervently than anyone else, yet in church he almost never did (preferring there to speak in a way all can understand), where did he speak in tongues? The only possible answer is that Paul exercised his remarkable gift in private, in the context of his personal, devotional intimacy with God.

Remember, this is the man who wrote Romans. This is the man whose incomparable mind and power of logical argumentation rendered helpless his theological opponents. This is the man who is known to history as the greatest theologian outside of Jesus himself. This is the man who took on and took out the philosophers in Athens (Acts 17)! Yes, logical, reasonable, highly-educated Paul prayed in tongues more than anyone!

Are Tongues a Sign?

The answer would appear to be yes, since 1 Corinthians 14:22 says, "tongues are for a sign." This follows Paul's quotation of Isaiah 28:11, "'By men of strange tongues and by the lips of strangers I will speak to this people, and even so they will not listen to me,' says the Lord." The meaning of this statement is found in a prior warning of God to Israel (Deut. 28:49). If Israel violated the covenant, God would chastise them by sending a foreign enemy, speaking a foreign tongue. The confusing and confounding speech was a sign of God's judgment. This is the judgment that Isaiah said had come upon Israel in the eighth century B.C. when the Assyrians invaded and conquered.[4]

What, then, is the principle that Paul found in Isaiah 28:11 that applied to Corinth (and to us)? It is this: when God speaks to people in a language they cannot understand, it is a form of punishment for unbelief. It signifies his anger. Incomprehensible speech will not guide or instruct or lead to faith and repentance, but only confuse and destroy. Thus, if outsiders or unbelievers come in and you speak in a language they cannot understand, you will simply drive them away. You will be giving unbelievers a sign that is entirely wrong—you are giving them a sign of severe judgment, but their hardness of heart has not reached the point where they deserve it. So Paul established these guidelines for when the church comes together (1 Cor. 14:26): if anyone speaks in a tongue, be sure there is an interpretation (v. 27). Otherwise the tongue-speaker should be quiet in the church (v. 28). Prophecy, on the other hand, is a sign of God's presence with believers (v. 22b), and should be used when unbelievers are present so they may see this sign and thereby come to Christian faith (vv. 24-25).

Therefore, Paul is *not* talking about the function of the gift of tongues in general, but only about the *negative* result of one particular *abuse* of tongues-speech (namely, its use without interpretation in the public assembly). So, uninterpreted tongues-speech should not be permitted in church, for in doing so, you run the risk of communicating a negative sign to people that will only drive them away.

Tongues in the Church

It would appear that some of the Corinthian believers had made two mistakes in their exercise of this gift. First, they had over-emphasized its importance, thinking that those who exercised a gift so obviously supernatural must themselves be extraordinarily favored of God. Their childish immaturity led them to conclude that tongues-speech was evidence of a transcendent and superior spirituality. Second, they were employing (indeed, flaunting) their tongues-speech in the public assembly without interpretation. Paul's response to such abuse was not to ban the gift of tongues from church life. Sinful, selfish abuse does not nullify the reality of a divine gift. His recommendation was not rejection, but correction.

Briefly, the apostle's counsel was twofold (vv. 26-40): Take steps to prevent a simultaneous cacophony of tongues-speech, and allow only two, or at most three, to speak during the course of a service. Why? (1) So the meeting does not become disorderly or unwieldy. (2) So that those with the gift of tongues would not assume a more prominent place in the body than was justified. The tongues-speaker should never think the gift is beyond control. The Holy Spirit does not compel or overwhelm. If the two or three had already spoken, Paul expected the others to keep quiet (implying that they had control/mastery over their gift). Paul would not accept the excuse: "But I just couldn't help myself. The presence and power and impulse of the Holy Spirit were just too much for me to contain. I would have been quenching the Spirit's work had I kept silent!" No. The Holy Spirit never moves or prompts someone to violate what he has previously said in Scripture.

I've already pointed to 1 Corinthians 14:14-19 as evidence that praying in tongues was a staple experience in Paul's private devotional life. This is confirmed by verse 28 where he gave instruction on what to do in the absence of an interpreter: "Let him [the tongues-speaker] speak to himself and to God." Where? Given the explicit prohibition of uninterpreted tongues-speech "in the church," it seems likely Paul had in mind prayer in tongues in private, a context other than the corporate gathering.

Some insist that Paul is instructing the tongues-speaker to pray silently to himself and to God while yet in the church gathering. But even if this were true (which I doubt), we would then have apostolic endorsement of *private* tongues-speech. If, as the cessationist contends, all tongues-speech is revelatory and is designed only for rational communication, Paul's counsel makes no sense. Why would God impart infallible, revelatory knowledge only for the recipient to speak it to himself and back to God? It seems as if the cessationist must envision the tongues-speaker waiting patiently until an interpreter arrives, at which time he can then speak audibly. But this is reading into the text a scenario conspicuous by its absence. Paul's instruction is for a situation in which there is no interpreter. He says nothing about the tongues-speaker waiting until one is present.

Furthermore, is it consistent with Paul's emphasis in 1 Corinthians 14 on all working together for mutual edification that he should recommend that some (perhaps many) focus their spiritual energy inwardly (praying in tongues) while someone else is speaking outwardly, ostensibly to edify the very people who on Paul's advice aren't even paying attention?

What About Corporate Singing in the Spirit?

One question I'm often asked, for which I don't have a definitive answer, is whether it is biblically permissible to sing in
uninterpreted tongues in a corporate setting. Many would
immediately say no and point to Paul's statement: "But if there
is no interpreter, let him [the tongues-speaker] keep silent in
the church; and let him speak to himself and to God [presum-
ably, in private]" (1 Cor. 14:28).

Of one thing I'm sure. If the corporate gathering in view is
an official church service, the point of which is to edify the body
(1 Cor. 14:26), uninterpreted tongues is not permissible. This
is what accounts for Paul's demand for silence in verse 28. But
what if the gathering is one at which only believers are in attendance? What if the purpose is not instruction or exhortation but
praise and intercession? One of Paul's concerns is that uninterpreted tongues will confuse any unbelievers who may be present
(vv. 22-23). But if it is a "believers" meeting, perhaps even a
small-group gathering in someone's home, that possibility no
longer exists. In such settings, the unintelligibility of uninterpreted tongues is no obstacle to achieving the purpose for
which people have congregated and therefore would not violate
Paul's counsel.

As I said, this isn't a definitive answer. I also realize that it
is, in large measure, an argument from silence. I'm only suggesting that we be cautious about enforcing the rules of
1 Corinthians 14 in contexts that Paul didn't envision or in circumstances other than those which evoked his inspired counsel.
What I'm saying is this. Some meetings today are of a decidedly
different nature and purpose from the meeting Paul had in view
in 1 Corinthians 14. There are meetings, for example, where the
overt aim and advertisement is *not* the instructional edification

of the body. Since this is a meeting at which the presence of unbelievers is neither encouraged nor expected, the effect of uninterpreted tongues, against which Paul warns in this chapter, is a moot point. If there were a gathering of Christians exclusively for the purpose of worship and prayer, a gathering in which the circumstances that evoked Paul's prohibition of uninterpreted tongues did not apply, would the prohibitions stand? I'm inclined to think not.

My Experience With Tongues

My first encounter with the gifts of the Spirit came when I was nineteen years old, in the summer of 1970. I was living in Lake Tahoe, Nevada, serving with Campus Crusade for Christ on an evangelistic project.

A friend of mine invited me to a meeting at which Harald Bredesen, one of the early leaders of the charismatic movement, was scheduled to speak. What Bredesen said that night sparked in me a desire for this gift. I began to pray earnestly to God that, if the gift were real, and in accordance with his will, he might give it to me. My determination was so intense that for several weeks I spent each night in a secluded area near my fraternity house at the University of Oklahoma pleading with God for some indication of his will for me concerning this gift.

One night, quite without warning, my prayer in English was interrupted by words of uncertain sound and form. I distinctly remember a somewhat detached sensation, as if I were separate from the one speaking. I had never experienced anything remotely similar to that in all my life. I kept thinking to myself, "Sam, what are you saying? Are you speaking in tongues?" I was both frightened and exhilarated. The experience lasted only a couple of minutes, but I felt closer to God and he to me than ever before.

I returned to my fraternity house filled with excitement and called a friend to tell him what had happened. Thirty minutes later I sat down in his car and said, "You'll never guess what happened tonight."

"You spoke in tongues, didn't you?" he asked, almost deadpan.

"Yes! It was great. But I don't understand what it means."

This person cared deeply for me and had no intention of offending me or obstructing my Christian growth. But what he said next affected me for years to come. "Sam, you realize, don't you, that if people find out about this you'll likely be excluded from any leadership position on campus. And I hate to say it, but a lot of people will think you're demonized."

I was crushed. I remember feebly, and with more than a little fear, trying to speak in tongues the next night, but nothing happened. Not wanting to forfeit my position in the ministry on campus, I concluded that it must have been something other than the Holy Spirit. I explained it away as a momentary emotional outburst that I'd be better off forgetting and not mentioning to anyone else. I never spoke of the incident or spoke in tongues again for twenty years!

In November of 1990, I was with Jack Deere in New Orleans at a theology conference. I shared with him what had happened back in the fall of 1970. He then reminded me of something the apostle Paul said to young Timothy: "And for this reason I remind you to *kindle afresh the gift of God* which is in you through the laying on of my hands" (2 Tim. 1:6). Jack then laid hands on me and asked the Lord to kindle afresh in me this gift he had bestowed on me so many years before.

This verse in 2 Timothy is important. As I indicated earlier in this book, it tells us that one may receive a spiritual gift only to neglect and ignore it. The imagery Paul uses is helpful. He describes a spiritual gift in terms of a flame that needs to be continually fanned. If it is not understood and nurtured and utilized in the way God intended, the once brightly burning flame can be reduced to a smoldering ember. "Take whatever steps you must take: study, pray, seek God's face, put it into practice, but by all means stoke the fire until that gift returns to its original intensity."

I took Paul's advice to Timothy and applied it to my own case. Every day, if only for a few minutes, I prayed that God would renew what he had given but I had quenched. I prayed that, if it were his will, I would once more be able to pray in the Spirit, to speak that heavenly language that would praise and thank and bless him (1 Cor. 14:2, 16-17). I didn't wait for some sort of divine seizure, but in faith began simply to speak forth the syllables and words that he brought to mind. Some twelve years have passed now since God renewed his precious gift in my life.

Praying in the Spirit is by no means the most important gift. Neither is it a sign of a spirituality or maturity greater than that of those who do not have this particular gift. But if no less a man than the apostle Paul can say, "I thank God, I speak in tongues more than you all" (1 Cor. 14:18), who am I to despise this blessed gift of God?

NINE

Tongues and Interpretation in the Church

Are tongues human languages? This is a key question for those who say the gift of tongues has ceased for today.

To answer that question, a study was conducted of people who claimed to speak in tongues. The conclusion was that rarely, if ever, did any of the subjects speak in what we know to be human dialects.[1] Cessationists have made much of this study because they feel it supports their premise that the gift of tongues has ceased. Their reasoning is quite simple: (a) all tongues in the New Testament were identified as human language; (b) no tongues today are human language; therefore (c) tongues are no longer a gift bestowed upon the church by the Holy Spirit.

I don't intend to discuss whether the study is right or wrong, although I have anecdotal evidence that challenges it. For example, I have spoken to many who tell of undeniable instances, often on the mission field, in which a believer spoke in a genuine human language without any previous exposure to it or study of it. I am inclined to believe them. But the more important issue is whether the initial premise of the cessationist is correct. That is to say, is it true that "all tongues in the New Testament were human language"?

Acts 2 is the only text in the New Testament where tongues-speech consists of foreign languages not previously known by the speaker. This is an important text, yet there is no reason to think Acts 2, rather than, say, 1 Corinthians 14, is the standard by which all occurrences of tongues-speech must be judged. Other factors suggest that tongues could also be heavenly or angelic speech.

To begin, if tongues-speech is always in a foreign language intended as a sign for unbelievers, why are the tongues in Acts 10 and Acts 19 spoken in the presence of only believers? Note also that Paul describes various kinds [or "species"[2]] of tongues (*genēglōssōn*) in 1 Corinthians 12:10. It is unlikely that he means a variety of different human languages, for who ever would have argued that all tongues were only one human language, such as Greek or Hebrew or German? His words suggest that there are differing categories of tongues-speech, perhaps human languages and heavenly languages.

Paul asserted that whoever speaks in a tongue "does not speak to men, but to God" (1 Cor. 14:2). But if tongues are always human languages, Paul is mistaken, for "speaking to men" is precisely what a human language does! If tongues-speech is always a human language, how could Paul say that "no one understands" (1 Cor. 14:2)? If tongues are human languages, many could potentially understand, as they did on the day of Pentecost (Acts 2:8-11). This would especially be true in Corinth, a multilingual cosmopolitan port city that was frequented by people of numerous dialects.

Moreover, if tongues-speech always is in a human language, then the gift of interpretation would be one for which no special work or enablement or manifestation of the Spirit would be required. Anyone who was multilingual, such as Paul, could interpret tongues-speech simply by virtue of education.

Furthermore, Paul referred to "tongues of men and of angels" (1 Cor. 13:1). While he may have been using hyperbole, he just as likely may have been referring to heavenly or angelic dialects for which the Holy Spirit gives utterance. Gordon Fee cited evidence in certain ancient Jewish sources that the angels were believed to have their own heavenly languages or dialects and that by means of the Spirit one could speak them.[3] In particular, we take note of the *Testament of Job*, where Job's three daughters put on heavenly sashes given to them as an inheritance from their father, by which they are transformed and enabled to praise God with hymns in angelic languages (see chapters 48 to 50). Some have questioned this account, however, pointing out that this section of the Testament may have been the work of a later Christian author. Yet, as Forbes points out, "What the Testament does provide ... is clear evidence that the concept of angelic languages as a mode of praise to God was an acceptable one within certain circles. As such it is our nearest parallel to *glossolalia*" [speaking in tongues].[4]

Some say the reference in 1 Corinthians 14:10-11 to earthly, foreign languages proves that all tongues-speech is also human languages. But the point of the analogy is that tongues function like foreign languages, not that tongues are foreign languages. Paul's point is that the hearer cannot understand uninterpreted tongues any more than he can understand the one speaking a foreign language. If tongues were a foreign language, there would be no need for an analogy.

Paul's statement in 1 Corinthians 14:18 that he "speaks in tongues more than you all" is evidence that tongues are not foreign languages. As Grudem noted, "If they were known foreign languages that foreigners could understand, as at Pentecost, why would Paul speak more than all the Corinthians in private, where no one would understand, rather than in church where foreign visitors could understand?"[5] Finally, if tongues-speech is always human language, Paul's statement in 1 Corinthians 14:23

wouldn't necesarily hold true. Any unbeliever who would know the language being spoken would more likely conclude the person speaking was highly educated rather than "mad."

What Is the Purpose of Tongues-Speech?

If we look carefully at what Paul says in 1 Corinthians 12 to 14 we can discern several reasons why God has bestowed this gift on his children.

(1) *Speaking in tongues is primarily a form of prayer* (1 Cor. 14:2), as I've already indicated. It is a means of communicating with God in supplication, petition, and intercession. If Ephesians 6:18 has tongues in view, then tongues are also a weapon in our arsenal for spiritual warfare.

Insofar as tongues are prayer, one might expect that God would sovereignly use this gift in any number of different contexts to accomplish his purposes. I am thinking in particular of the way God has used tongues in the ministry of Jackie Pullinger.[6]

Jackie was only five years old when she first sensed the call of God on her life. As she grew to adulthood the message became even clearer—"Go!"

"Where, Lord?"

"Go, trust me, and I will lead you."

Rebuffed and turned down by every missionary organization she contacted (no one wanted a British musician who lacked proper missiological training), Jackie sought the advice of her pastor. "Well, if you've tried all the conventional ways and missionary societies and God is still telling you to go, you had better get on the move.... If I were you I would go out and buy a ticket for a boat going on the longest journey you can find and pray to know where to get off."

She did. Jackie Pullinger quite literally took "a slow boat to China" and for the past thirty-five years has been ministering in Hong Kong. The infamous Walled City, where Jackie set up shop, sat on only six-and-one-half acres of land but was home to upwards of 50,000 people! It was quite literally a world unto itself, with neither China nor Great Britain exercising proper jurisdiction. It was a haven for thieves, murderers, extortionists, drug lords, pornographers, illegal immigrants and refugees, the homeless, runaways, pimps, and prostitutes (many of whom were twelve- and thirteen-year-old girls, sold into the trade by neighbors, boyfriends, even parents). Pornographic theaters, as well as opium and heroin dens, lined the narrow walkways and alleys. The city was ruled by the Triads, Chinese secret societies which had degenerated into ruthless criminal gangs.

The filth was beyond belief. Open sewers, human refuse flowing freely in the streets, rats that no longer reacted to the shrill screams of frightened visitors. Bodies of addicts who over-dosed the night before were piled outside the city.

Into this nightmare walked a twenty-year-old girl from England who had no money, no job, and couldn't speak a word of Chinese. But she managed to learn enough to tell the heroin addicts about Jesus. Jackie first heard about the gift of tongues from a young Chinese couple. Not long after she began fervently praying in tongues during her devotional times, Jackie began to see an increase in conversions and healing miracles. But the most amazing thing was how God used this gift in helping heroin addicts during withdrawal.

Perhaps the greatest obstacle to deliverance from drugs is the indescribable and unbearable pain of withdrawal. The agony of going "cold-turkey" has driven the vast majority of addicts back to their habit. But Jackie made a startling discovery. It was her custom for her new converts to be filled with the Holy Spirit and to receive a prayer language. They always did. But then she observed that when the pain of withdrawal would begin, it would just as quickly end if the individual would begin praying in tongues! It took a while to convince a few of the converts, but the horrors of withdrawal made them desperate. As Jackie and others would pray for them in tongues, they too would cry out to God in their new language. Miraculously, and virtually without exception, each one came off drugs without the wrenching pain associated with this experience.

Most of these addicts had been on heroin or opium for years and had quite literally run out of space on their bodies in which to inject themselves with the drug. Their lives were controlled by their addiction, and few would hesitate to steal or even kill to support their habit. Many had sold friends and family members into prostitution to keep the flow of drugs coming. Yet when they converted to faith in Jesus and prayed in tongues, the power of addiction was defeated!

(2) *Speaking in tongues is a means for edifying oneself* (1 Cor. 14:4). Far from being sinful or selfish, self-edification is a command we are to obey: "But you, beloved, building yourselves up on your most holy faith; praying in the Holy Spirit ..." (Jude 20).

(3) *Speaking in tongues is a form of blessing the person and works of God* (1 Cor. 14:16). Hence, tongues-speech is a form of *praise* (especially "singing in the spirit"). As Jack Hayford has pointed out, there comes a time when those who press in to the heart of God in worship "reach a place of acknowledged limitation."[7] We simply must break through the restrictions of earthly speech and song if we are to express our heart's deepest desires and passions. Singing in the Spirit serves this end and enables us to consummate our praise in a way that little else can.

(4) *Speaking in tongues is a way of giving thanks to God* (1 Cor. 14:16). When we pray or sing in the Spirit we are expressing our gratitude for the many blessings of salvation and life we have in Christ.

(5) *Speaking in tongues is a way of compensating for our weakness and ignorance in praying for ourselves and others* (Rom. 8:26-27). For example, we can pray in tongues when our minds wander and we struggle to focus or concentrate, or when we are physically tired and weary, or when we are distracted by people and the noise around us. When we think we've run out of things to pray for ("what's left?") or when things to pray for are not readily coming to mind, we can pray in the Spirit. When we don't know someone's pain or problem or when we feel inadequate to intercede for them, we may pray in tongues, confident that the Holy Spirit will articulate through us to the Father precisely their most urgent needs. Thus tongues forever eliminate the excuse for not praying: "But I don't know what to say."

Why Is Tongues-Speech Often So Rapid?

People often ask this question. Either they have heard others pray in tongues with great rapidity or they themselves have experienced this phenomenon. I can't be dogmatic, for the Scriptures don't address the issue. But perhaps it is because the Holy Spirit is praying through us and thus prayer in tongues entails a higher level of spiritual energy (Acts 2:4; 1 Cor. 14: 14-15). Also, since it is the Holy Spirit who is articulating our prayers, there is no hesitation over which words to speak; no stammering or wondering what to say and how to say it; no uh's punctuating our speech; none of the fear or self-consciousness that characterizes and thus retards normal speaking. When praying in tongues one need never "wait" to think of something to say.

Why Are People So Afraid of Tongues? Why Are They So Hesitant to Pursue and Practice It?

Again, let me suggest several reasons. First of all, Christians who were raised and nurtured in strong, Bible-based churches are extraordinarily fearful of the slightest artificiality in Christian experience. They demand a virtual guarantee, in advance, that what they do will be genuine. Often this caution is born of a fear that inevitably paralyzes faith, as well as the willingness to try and to risk. After first speaking in what they hope is tongues, the slightest doubt of its authenticity prompts them never to try again. I believe in being passionate for what is genuine, but we must not let fear of artificiality control our lives.

Another factor is that often, after first speaking in tongues, people conclude that it didn't *feel* sufficiently supernatural. It didn't seem significantly different from what it takes to pray in English. So either it wasn't real or it isn't worth the effort.

The initial experience with tongues often doesn't sound like a language. It seems like irrational and incoherent gibberish. "How could something so trite and repetitious be of any spiritual value?" people ask. Such disillusionment leads to their abandoning the practice altogether.

Finally, many shy away from tongues for fear of "sounding silly." Appearing foolish in the presence of people whose respect and love you cherish can often paralyze one's passion for this spiritual gift.

Advice for Those Who Do Not Speak in Tongues

I think it best to conclude with seven comments, designed especially for those who do not have this gift but perhaps feel a tug in their hearts to ask for it.

(1) *You don't have to be afraid.* Many people have been frightened off with warnings of receiving a counterfeit or—worse still—of opening themselves to demonic influence. Yet the apostle Paul never gave any warning about counterfeit tongues. The church at Corinth was filled with recently converted men and women whose background was characterized by pagan and demonic rituals. It was to these very people that Paul said, "I wish that you all spoke in tongues" (1 Cor. 14:5)! Nowhere does Paul say or suggest, "I want you all to be afraid of tongues." Paul's counsel is well-grounded, for it was Jesus who said:

> "Now suppose one of you fathers is asked by his son for a fish; he will not give him a snake instead of a fish, will he? Or if he is asked for an egg, he will not give him a scorpion, will he? If you then, being evil, know how to give good gifts to your children, how much more shall your heavenly Father give the Holy Spirit to those who ask Him?"
>
> LUKE 11:11-13

(2) *You will not lose control.* Some are reluctant to follow the Spirit's prompting to speak in a prayer language for fear that they will lose control of themselves and do something foolish or embarrassing or irreverent. But as we have seen, those who speak in tongues are never described in Scripture as losing control of their faculties or falling under the influence of an irresistible

power. The purpose of tongues is not to overwhelm or humiliate you but to bless God, bless others, and edify your own soul. Remember, there is no safer place to be than under the control of the Spirit of God.

(3) *You don't have to join a charismatic church.* If God should grant you this gift, you can still continue your life in your present church home. The only thing that might change is the amount of time you spend in prayer and the freedom and joy you begin to experience in worship.

However, I should warn you that you may well encounter opposition and even ridicule from some who will dismiss your experience as either madness or demonic influence. Don't be defensive. Be patient and loving with them and allow time for the fruit of this gift to grow. It may prove helpful to seek support and encouragement in a small Bible study group or home prayer fellowship sponsored by another church that is attended by believers who embrace the gifts of the Spirit.

You may also encounter the charge: "Oh, I guess this means you think you're better than we are. You're the 'have' and we're the 'have-nots.'" This is a tragic misunderstanding not only of the gift of tongues but of our relationship to the work of the Spirit in general. Simply reassure them as gently but firmly as possible that the gift of tongues has *not* made you a better Christian than they. Perhaps the best way to respond is by saying: "I don't believe that I am now a better Christian than you. I simply believe that I am now on my way to being a better Christian than I was before I received this gift." God forbids us to compare ourselves with others, as if we, because of a particular gift, were better than they (1 Cor. 4:7). But it is an essential part of the Christian life that we grow up in our faith and deepen in our devotion to Jesus through the increase and expansion of the Spirit's work in our lives.

(4) *You don't have to put your brain on ice.* Praying and singing in tongues is in no way incompatible with a love for the written Word of God and the deep things of theology. Speaking in tongues does not turn your "gray matter" to mush nor diminish the importance of solid doctrine in your life.

I can only speak for myself here, but my love for the Scriptures has only grown deeper since receiving this gift. If those who pray and praise in tongues find themselves less and less inclined to dig deeply into the theological treasures of the Word, it is not because of the gift of tongues. If there were a connection between *glossolalia* and disdain for doctrine, surely Paul would have informed (and warned) us of it. And let us never forget that it was the apostle Paul, author of the epistle to the Romans and other doctrinal treatises, who said, "I thank God I speak in tongues more than you all!"

(5) *If you don't speak in tongues, but want to, you don't have to prime the pump by repeatedly saying* banana *backwards.* Ignore those who might be tempted to suggest certain words to you if you are having a hard time getting started. It is the Spirit who gives utterance (Acts 2:4), not a well-meaning friend. Speaking in tongues is not an experience of "oral seizure," as if God intends to perform a miraculous jiggling of your mouth and lips. Simply wait upon the Lord and speak forth the words he brings to mind, no matter how incoherent or silly they may sound. They are sweet music to your Father's ear.

(6) *Persevere in prayer.* When Paul exhorted us to earnestly desire spiritual gifts, he intended us to ask God for what is our heart's desire. Don't be ashamed of wanting this gift. And don't be discouraged if the answer isn't quick in coming. If the ultimate answer is no, then rejoice in the gifts God has already given and use them to his glory and the edification of the church.

Not long ago I received a letter from a highly educated and widely respected lady concerning her own experience with tongues. Here is an excerpt from it:

For what its worth, let me quickly relate my own tongues experience. Twenty years ago, in high school, my wild and crazy Pentecostal boyfriend and his Pentecostal cohorts tried every which way to get me—a conservative Baptist girl—to speak in tongues. I wasn't opposed to the idea, but try as they did (prayer, moaning, speaking in tongues over me ... everything short of slashing themselves with knives), nothing happened. They came to the conclusion that I was horribly unspiritual and resistant to God's work in my life. I can't say that I was deeply marred by the experience, but it did leave me feeling somewhat wary of the validity of the gift.

In June of this year [1995], the Spirit put on my heart the desire to enter an extended fast. On the fourth day (a really, really difficult day of battling against the physical and mental desire to eat) while I was pouring my heart out to God, foreign and strange words welled up from deep within and came spilling out of my mouth. It was quite a few moments before it dawned on me that I was speaking in tongues. Over the next days and weeks of the fast, I was able to use this gift to battle against severe temptation. I doubt whether I would have had the physical, mental, and spiritual strength to complete the fast without it. I felt as though the Spirit of God within was interceding to the Father on my behalf. The gift remains with me. I feel most moved to use it during times of deep intercession or deep praise. "Deep" is the best adjective I can think of—it is kind of hard to describe, but I think you know what I mean.

The interesting thing about this lady's experience is that she was not seeking the gift of tongues. She was simply seeking God ... with all her heart, soul, mind, and strength. I'm not suggesting that you must follow her example, nor that you will necessarily receive a new prayer language simply because you fast and pray. But you might!

(7) *Devote yourself to extended periods of praise.* I want to close with this simple suggestion. Set aside a time and place where you can be alone with the Lord for a few hours of uninterrupted meditation and worship. Whether or not you combine this with fasting is up to you. Put a praise tape in the cassette player and spend as much time as possible adoring the beauty of Christ and enjoying the joy of being enjoyed by him. Open your heart, open your mouth, and sing forth the love songs he has put within. What happens next is between you and God.

The Gift of Interpretation of Tongues

The interpretation of tongues may be the most neglected gift in the body of Christ. It is also one of the more important gifts, insofar as it alone makes possible the introduction of tongues-speech and its obvious blessings into the gathered assembly of believers. But before looking at what this gift is, let me explain what it *is not.*

What the Gift Is Not

This gift of interpreting tongues is not the ability to interpret revelation on a broad scale. Someone who has this gift does not automatically have the ability to interpret dreams, visions, or other revelatory phenomena.

Although not mentioned in the New Testament, there may

well be a charisma of *interpretation,* broadly conceived. Joseph attributed to God his ability to interpret dreams (Gen. 41:14-16), but so, too, would anyone who possessed any spiritual gift. Daniel was also enabled to interpret revelatory dreams (see Dan. 2, 4 and especially 5:14-16). The gift of interpretation (1 Cor. 12:10), on the other hand, does not stand alone, but is inextricably tied up with tongues.

This gift must be distinguished from the ability to translate a foreign language. All of us have seen translators at the United Nations, for example, where educated people interpret speeches for the representatives of various countries. This is an impressive skill, but it is a natural, learned, human ability that requires no supernatural anointing of God. Interpretation of tongues, on the other hand, is no less a "manifestation" (1 Cor. 12:7) of the Holy Spirit than the gift of miracles or prophecy.

What the Gift of Interpretation Is

The charisma of interpretation of tongues is *the Spirit-empowered ability to translate a public utterance of tongues into the language of the congregation.* The word *translate,* however, is somewhat ambiguous. There is a spectrum from literal translation at one end to broad summation at the other end, whenever the gift of interpretation is exercised.

Interpreting a tongues utterance might conceivably be a literal, word-for-word translation, equivalent in length to the utterance in tongues. Often what is said in tongues is enigmatic or parabolic or symbolic. This would require the interpreter to explain what was said and unpack its significance, not unlike what an art critic does when "interpreting" a painting and explaining its intent or mood.

Perhaps the gift of interpretation gives expression to a looser, more fluid rendering that captures the essence or gist of the utterance but falls well short of a word-for-word rendering. Or it may simply be a paraphrase of what was said.

I see no reason to think the Holy Spirit couldn't enable someone to interpret a tongues utterance anywhere along this spectrum. Thus someone might speak in tongues at great length while the interpretation is brief. It is entirely possible that one interpreter might provide a long, virtually word-for-word translation, while another provides a summarization of its basic content. In any case, the movement is always from the obscurity and unintelligibility of the tongues utterance to clarity and intelligibility of the interpretation, such that everyone in the church can say amen to what was said (1 Cor. 14:16). In this way the entire body is edified.

The Content of Interpretation

Earlier we noted that tongues can be any form of prayer (1 Cor. 14:2), or perhaps worship (1 Cor. 14:16; compared with Acts 2:11; 10:46), as well as thanksgiving (1 Cor. 14:16). Therefore interpretations will also take the form of prayers, praise, and expressions of gratitude to God. In other words, if the focus of tongues is God-ward, so too will be the interpretation.

This raises the question of whether there is any such thing as a *message* in tongues, in other words, a message directed horizontally to people rather than vertically to God. Pentecostal and charismatic believers have long assumed that when tongues are interpreted the result is the equivalent of prophecy. Mark Stibbe, however, rightly challenges this view, insisting that

> when a tongue is given in public, there is a sense in which the congregation is "overhearing" the passionate worship of an individual believer [much like what happens when we read the Psalms: these are hymns of praise from a

believer or the nation to God]. If an interpretation is offered which is not in the form of prayerful adoration, we should be cautious about regarding it as a genuine interpretation. If it is offered in the form of praise language, then it has a much better chance of being the true "interpretation."[8]

If the interpretation of tongues is nothing more than prophecy, why not just have prophetic words and not bother with the tongues? I agree that interpreted tongues *function* like prophecy insofar as they edify and encourage other believers (1 Cor. 14:5). But that is not to say interpreted tongues are identical with prophecy. The latter would be true only if one assumes (and then proves) that tongues-speech is revelatory.

If what I've said is correct, it would suggest that the many so-called messages in tongues directed to people in the form of instruction, rebuke, or exhortation have *not* been properly interpreted. Tongues + interpretation ≠ prophecy, but rather tongues + interpretation = prayer or praise or thanksgiving.

Conclusion

I wonder if perhaps the opposition to tongues and its interpretation comes less from careful exegesis of the New Testament than from reaction to the emotional dynamics so often linked to their exercise. But surely God can be trusted with our emotions no less than with our minds. It would appear that many affirm God's sovereign control over everything *except* their feelings. One of the things I've learned through my experience with spiritual gifts is that God can be trusted to direct and oversee our *experience* of his power no less than our theological *affirmation* of it.

Jack Hayford, pastor emeritus of Church on the Way in Van Nuys, California, has some helpful words of wisdom for us all. Hayford wrote:

> It began to dawn on me that, given an environment where the Word of God was foundational and the Person of Christ the focus, the Holy Spirit could be trusted to do both—enlighten the intelligence and ignite the emotions. I soon discovered that to allow him that much space necessitates more a surrender of my senseless fears than a surrender of sensible control. God is not asking any of us to abandon reason or succumb to some euphoric feeling. He is, however, calling us to trust him—enough to give him control.[9]

TEN

Letting Your Gift Find You

If you've come to this chapter having read the previous nine, congratulations! I say this because it demonstrates your concern for spiritual gifts and the role they play in your life as a believer and in the life of the church. It also demonstrates your commitment to the authority of Scripture. There are far too many Christians who just don't believe this issue is important enough to warrant the investment of time and energy to read another book. Often with a pained look on their faces, they ask, "Are spiritual gifts really *that* important?" I'll answer that question by asking a few of my own, each of which is drawn directly from what Paul says in the fourth chapter of Ephesians.

Do you think it's important for Christians to get along with each other? Do you value Christian unity? I assume you believe that oneness and mutual love and a common mind are crucial for the life of the church. Yet Paul said that if we hope to experience this "unity of the faith" we must have spiritual gifts (Eph. 4:13a) functioning in the way God designed them.

Do you believe it's important that Christians be spiritually equipped to do the work and fulfill the service apart from which the church cannot be built up (Eph. 4:12)? If so, spiritual gifts are essential.

Is knowing Jesus a vital part of the Christian life? I know it's a stupid question! But few realize that God "gave gifts to men" (Eph. 4:8), such as prophecy and teaching and the like, "until we attain to ... the knowledge of the Son of God" (Eph. 4:13). God has graciously given spiritual gifts to help us grow and deepen and expand and increase in our knowledge and enjoyment of "the unfathomable riches of Christ" (Eph. 3:8).

Most believers long for maturity and theological integrity and encouraging speech and growth. But few realize that these things are all tied to the proper exercise of spiritual gifts in the life of the church (Eph. 4:13-16).

Simply put, there is little hope that the chasm I referred to in chapter one will ever be bridged if we continue to neglect spiritual gifts or relegate them to a secondary status in the body of Christ. So, if you persevered long enough to reach this point in the book, I say again, congratulations!

I hope this book has generated some excitement in your heart about the prospects of seeing the power of God manifested in the gifts he has made available. But I imagine some of you are unsure of what to do next, perhaps even scared of what the future might hold if you were to begin practicing these spiritual gifts in your personal life. Perhaps you're a pastor and don't know how to incorporate these ideas into the life of your congregation. I don't have a magical agenda that works perfectly for everyone, but I do have a few suggestions in closing.

First of all, honestly and openly face the fact that you are more controlled by fear than you either know or are willing to admit. It's OK. We all are when we first start out. A lot of spiritual veterans are too. There are all sorts of fears that grip the soul when the subject of spiritual gifts and supernatural power is introduced into the church.

- Fear of being associated with people whose behavior, dress, mannerisms, and style of ministry are embarrassing
- Fear of losing the respect of your peers (will they ever again ask me out to lunch once they discover I speak in tongues?)

- Fear of the unknown and unfamiliar
- Fear of losing whatever reinforces one's sense of peace, comfort, "rightness"
- Fear of what you can't predict or control
- Fear of losing the good things about church life you've worked hard to achieve
- Fear of losing control of your church and of your own emotions, just to mention a fe

It's important that you talk about these fears with others who share them. I encourage you to spend time openly discussing them in small groups. Be honest about why you are afraid. Dig deeply into your own soul about the underlying cause. Spend time in prayer with one another asking God to reveal any hidden motives or pride or personal agendas that might account for your hesitancy to obey Scripture concerning the use of these gifts. Once these fears and their causes have been identified, they are much easier to overcome.

Second, if you are a leader in your church, cultivate an atmosphere, through both teaching and personal example, in which people in your church or small group can fail safely. If people fear open rebuke or censure, it's unlikely they will step out in faith to exercise the gifts God has given them. People are terrified of incurring the disdain of their leaders. They are afraid of being disciplined or abandoned, of being left alone with no covering or protection. In such cases they will rarely take risks in praying for the sick or in speaking what they think God has revealed to them.

But do more than tell them it's OK to fail. If and when they do fail, encourage them to try again. Reassure them that they haven't failed God or the church or the individual to whom they were trying to minister. I especially encourage leaders themselves to openly acknowledge their own failures. If people know and see that their pastor or elders or group leaders aren't afraid to risk making a mistake, they will find new strength to follow the prompting of the Spirit and use the gifts God has bestowed.

Third, make a decision not to let your lack of experience set your personal or corporate or ecclesiastical agenda. Don't excuse your disobedience to Scripture by appealing to the fact that you've never tried these things before or never seen others do so successfully. The people who are most resistant to the supernatural work of the Spirit are often the people who are least experienced or who have been offended by others who messed up. But everyone has to start at some point. You can't jump into the exercise of spiritual gifts as a seasoned veteran who always knows how to avoid looking dumb! God isn't asking you to be perfect. He's simply asking you to be obedient.

Fourth, embrace the fact that spiritual renewal is almost always messy. There is no such thing as a work of God in and through humans without stumbling blocks and mistakes. The activity of the Holy Spirit is never as tidy and neat and precise as we expect it to be. If you attitude is: "Well, I'll wait until it gets cleaned up and orderly and error-free and compatible with what makes me feel comfortable," you'll never get started at all.

I've often heard people express their concerns about opening their churches to the supernatural activity of the Spirit lest they become disorderly and chaotic like ancient Corinth. But as J. I. Packer has pointed out, "many churches today are orderly simply because they are asleep, and with some one fears that it is the sleep of death. It is no great thing to have order in a cemetery. The real and deplorable carnality and immaturity of the Corinthian Christians, which Paul censures so strongly elsewhere in the letter, must not blind us to the fact that they were enjoying the ministry of the Holy Spirit in a way in which we today are not."[1]

Fifth, and finally, provide detailed, intensive, and oft-repeated biblical instruction on the foundation and function of the gifts. Don't just teach on it once. Read extensively and arrange for opportunities for people to ask questions and to pray for one another.

So, What's My Gift?

The answer to our final question is not found in a spiritual gifts inventory or personality profile. If I sound a bit skeptical about such things, I am. I think Scripture would have us take a far more practical, almost pragmatic, approach to discovering our spiritual gifts, an approach that is at its heart need-based. Let me give you some examples of what I mean.

The next time you're in church or in a small group or just hanging out with other believers, pause momentarily and ask: Is anyone physically hurt or suffering from chronic pain? If so, take your hands out of your pockets, lay them on your brother or sister, and pray for God's healing power.

Is anyone you know distraught or discouraged? Are some finding life too frustrating to bear? If so, take them out for a cup of coffee and listen to their story. You don't have to theologize about their predicament. They're not looking for explanations. They just want someone who cares enough to spend a few minutes with them. Just listen to them. Then love them.

Is anyone struggling financially with few prospects to get them out of the hole? Do something courageous. Give them your last fifty dollars and trust God to supply your need.

Is anyone confused about some verse of Scripture they just read in their devotional time? Perhaps you're just as befuddled as they are. Pull out a concordance, a study Bible, perhaps a commentary from the church library, and study a bit. Then sit down with your friend and put your heads (and hearts) together and pray for the Spirit to shed light on your thinking.

Is anyone struggling with sin? (Well, of course they are!) Offer to pray for them. But before you do, sit quietly together and ask the Lord to guide your thoughts and speak words of wisdom to your soul. If you sense something, or a thought comes to mind, share it with them. It might be the key that opens the door to their hearts and brings freedom from bondage.

Does the person you just prayed for report hearing voices in their head? Do they struggle with paralyzing shame, virtually bombarded on a daily basis by accusing thoughts and self-contempt? If so, speak the Word of God over them with authority. In the name of Christ, command any demonic spirits to leave and never to return. Pray for them to be filled afresh with the Holy Spirit.

Is anyone overwhelmed by the clutter in their garage and that ever-increasing mountain of dirty laundry? Offer to spend Saturday with them, helping out, picking up, washing, drying, folding, and putting away clothes.

None of this sounds especially spectacular. (Well, maybe some of it does.) So what am I getting at with these questions? Simply this. If we spend less time searching to identify our spiritual gift(s) and more time actually praying and giving and helping and teaching and serving and exhorting those around us, the likelihood greatly increases that we will walk headlong into our gifting without ever knowing what happened. God will more likely meet us with his gifts in the midst of trying to help his children than he ever would while we're taking a spiritual gifts analysis test.

I earlier raised the question of whether there might be spiritual gifts beyond those explicitly mentioned in the New Testament. I'm inclined to believe that there are potentially as many gifts as there are needs in the life of the church and in the experience of individual Christians.

So, look for a need and meet it. Find a hurt and heal it. Be alert to the cry for help and answer it. Listen for the voice of God and speak it. Identify someone's weakness and overcome it. Look for what's missing and supply it. When you do, the power of God—the energizing, enabling, charismatic activity of the Holy Spirit—will equip you, perhaps only once, but possibly forever, to minister hope and encouragement to those in need. So, if you're still wondering what your gift(s) might be, act first and ask later.

NOTES

ONE

When Power Comes to Church

1. For an extensive treatment of this issue, see my contribution to the book *Are Miraculous Gifts for Today? Four Views* (Grand Rapids, Mich.: Zondervan, 1996), edited by Wayne Grudem, as well as Jack Deere's book *Surprised by the Power of the Spirit* (Grand Rapids, Mich.: Zondervan, 1993). A more technical treatment of some of what I discuss in this book may be found in the *Four Views* volume.
2. On this issue, see Deere, *Surprised by the Power of the Spirit*, 58–71, 229–52.

TWO

Right? Wrong!

1. The word *pneumatikōn* may be taken in one of two ways. It may be masculine in gender and refer to "spiritual people" (1 Cor. 2:15; 3:1; 14:37; Gal. 6:1), or it may be neuter and refer to "spiritual things," such as (but not restricted to) spiritual gifts (1 Cor. 9:11; 12:1; 14:1). In Ephesians 6:12 *pneumatikōn* is neuter and refers to demonic spirits.
2. Gordon Fee, *God's Empowering Presence: The Holy Spirit in the Letters of Paul* (Peabody, Mass.: Hendrickson, 1994), 773. Emphasis added.

3. Jack Deere, *The Beginner's Guide to the Gift of Prophecy* (Ann Arbor, Mich.: Servant, 2001), 34.

4. I'm not entirely convinced that apostleship is a spiritual gift, at least not in the same way the other phenomena discussed in this book are. I discuss this in the book *Are Miraculous Gifts for Today?*, 156-59.

THREE
Words of Wisdom and Knowledge

1. James D.G. Dunn, *Jesus and the Spirit* (Philadelphia: Westminster, 1975), 217.

2. Dunn, 217.

3. See 1 Corinthians 1:18-27 where in the span of these ten verses the word *wisdom* and its derivatives occur twelve times! In 1 Corinthians 2:1 Paul said that when he preached to the Corinthians it was not with "superiority of speech (*logos*) or of wisdom (*sophia*)" [interestingly, the same Greek terms used in 1 Cor. 12:8], but rather "in demonstration of the Spirit and of power" (2:4). See also 2:5-8, 13 for additional references and allusions to wisdom. Especially noteworthy is 1 Corinthians 1:17 where Paul said that Christ did not send him to proclaim the gospel "in cleverness (*sophia*, i.e., wisdom!) of speech (*logos*)." Again in 2:4 Paul insisted he did not preach with persuasive "words (*logos*) of wisdom (*sophia*)." The same two words are found together yet again in 2:13.

4. Mark Stibbe, *Know Your Spiritual Gifts* (London: Marshall Pickering, 1997), 22. Emphasis added.

5. Stibbe, 49.

6. Dunn, 220.

7. Dunn, 218.

8. Dunn, 221.

9. See Wayne Grudem, *Systematic Theology: An Introduction to Biblical Doctrine* (Grand Rapids, Mich.: Zondervan, 1994), 1080-82.

10. Charles H. Spurgeon, *Autobiography: Volume 2, The Full Harvest, 1860-1892* (Edinburgh, Scotland: Banner of Truth Trust, 1973), 60.

11. Jack Deere tells much of Paul Cain's life story in his book, *The Beginner's Guide to the Gift of Prophecy.*

FOUR
Faith and Healing

1. Stibbe, 58-66.

2. Donald A. Carson, *Showing the Spirit: A Theological Exposition of 1 Corinthians* (Grand Rapids, Mich.: Baker, 1987), 39.

3. Carson, 39.

4. For a refutation of this argument, see my discussion in the book *Are Miraculous Gifts for Today?*, 186-90.

5. See Matthew 8:15; 9:18-25, 27-31; 14:36; 17:7; 19:13-15; Mark 1:40-42; 5:21-24; 6:1-6, 56; 7:31-35; 8:22-25; 9:27; 16:18; Luke 13:10-13; 22:51. Also note the practice of the early church in Acts 3:7; 5:12; 6:6; 8:17-19; 9:10-17, 41; 13:1-3; 14:3; 19:11; 28:7-8. This emphasis is also found in 1 Timothy 4:14; 5:22; 2 Timothy 1:6 (cf. Deut. 34:9; Num. 27:15-23).

6. The first person I heard articulate this principle was my friend Jack Taylor.

FIVE
It's a Miracle!

1. Also, the word translated "works" (*erga*) is frequently used (especially in John) to describe the miraculous deeds of Jesus (see John 5:20, 36[2]; 7:21, a reference to the miracle of 5:2ff.; 9:3-4; 10:25, 32[2], 33, 37-38). Other occurrences of *work/s* in John which refer either to the works of men or the general/overall activity of God include 3:19-21; 4:34; 6:28-29; 7:3, 7; 8:39, 41; 15:24; 17:4. The other three references to works are those in John 14:10-12.

2. Max Turner, *The Holy Spirit and Spiritual Gifts in the New Testament Church and Today*, rev. ed. (Peabody, Mass.: Hendrickson, 1998), 272.

3. Grudem, *Systematic Theology*, 355.

4. Philip Yancey, "Jesus, the Reluctant Miracle Worker" *Christianity Today*, May 19, 1997, 80.

5. John Piper, "The Signs of the Apostle," *The Standard*, November 1991, 28.

6. Wayne Grudem has responded to this argument at great length in an article titled, "Should Christians Expect Miracles Today?" in *The Kingdom and the Power*, ed. by Gary S. Greig and Kevin N. Springer (Ventura, Calif.: Regal, 1993), 55-110 (esp. 91-95).

7. The closest was Lexell's Comet in 1770, which came within 1.5 million miles of the Earth.

8. Fred Schaff, *Comet of the Century: From Halley to Hale-Bopp* (New York: Copernicus, 1997), 16.

9. Information concerning the extent of the drought was obtained from the National Climatic Data Center in Asheville, North Carolina, and the Kansas City

International Airport Weather Station. The only summer drier than that of 1983 was in 1976 when seven one-hundredths of an inch (.07) less rainfall was recorded for Kansas City. The U.S. Department of Agriculture issued a summary of crop production with a review of the growing season and the weather. They described the summer of 1983 as a "record-breaking heat wave," one result of which was a drop of over 28% in the corn yield from the previous year.

SIX
Prophecy and Distinguishing of Spirits

1. *The Autobiography of Charles H. Spurgeon*, vol. 2 (Curts & Jennings, 1899), 226-27.
2. *The Autobiography of Charles H. Spurgeon*, vol. 2, 226-27.
3. Grudem, *Systematic Theology*, 121-22.

SEVEN
Who Said God Said?

1. In 1 Thessalonians 5:20, the NASB speaks of "prophetic utterances" and the NIV has "prophecies." Literally, this is the plural form of the word *prophecy* and refers not so much to the gift of prophecy but to the individual utterances or words that come forth in the life of a church.
2. Much of my discussion of this passage is dependent on Wayne Grudem's excellent book, *The Gift of Prophecy in the New Testament and Today*, rev. ed. (Wheaton, Ill.: Crossway, 2000). See especially 54-62.

3. Some insist "the others" are the "other prophets." However, the term Paul uses for "others" (*hoi alloi*) usually means "others different from the subject," i.e., people other than the prophets whose utterances are to be evaluated (i.e., the others who make up the larger group; i.e., the congregation as a whole). If Paul meant "the rest" of the prophets present at the meeting he would more likely have used a different term (*hoi loipoi*), which carries the meaning "the rest of the same class." It could be Paul was referring to those who have the gift of "distinguishing of spirits" (12:10). In 1 Cor. 12:10 the word translated "distinguishing" is the noun *diakrisis*. In 14:29 the word translated "pass judgment" is the related verb form *diakrino*. Supporting this view is the fact that "distinguishing of spirits" in 12:10 appears to be coupled with the gift of prophecy in much the same way "interpretation" is coupled with the gift of tongues. But then why wouldn't Paul simply have said, "And let those who distinguish between spirits pass judgment," if in fact he had such a group in mind? Also, if we take "the others" to refer either to a special group of prophets or those with the gift of discerning spirits, what is the majority of the congregation to do when prophecies are being uttered and evaluated? It seems they would be compelled to sit passively waiting for the proph-ecy to end and be judged before knowing whether to believe it or not. Furthermore, these first two views would require us to believe that teachers, pastors, and other church leaders without either the gift of prophecy or discerning spirits must sit passively awaiting the verdict of an elite group. None of this seems plausible.

4. Grudem, *The Gift of Prophecy*, 57. Max Turner concurs: "Here [in 1 Cor. 14:29], clearly, it is not a matter of deciding

whether it is true prophecy or false prophecy, and then stoning the prophet (or at least exorcising her) in the latter case. It is a matter of deciding what is from God, and how it applies, and of separating this from what is merely human inference. Indeed, the human element and human error appears to have been so apparent that in 1 Thessalonians 5:19, 20 Paul has to warn the congregation, 'Do not despise prophecies, but test everything; hold fast to what is good.' Arguably, then, prophecy in the New Testament is thus a mixed phenomenon" (*Holy Spirit and Spiritual Gifts*, 214).

EIGHT
What Is the Gift of Tongues?

1. See Acts 2:37-42, 8:26-40; 9:1-19; 13:44-52; 16:11-15, 25-34; 17:1-33; 18:1-11.
2. Gordon Fee, *The First Epistle to the Corinthians* (Grand Rapids, Mich.: Eerdmans, 1987), 657. Emphasis added.
3. Jack Hayford, *The Beauty of Spiritual Language* (Dallas, Tex.: Word, 1992), 102-6.
4. Also compare with God's judgment upon Israel in the sixth century B.C., recorded in Jer. 5:15.

NINE
Tongues and Interpretation in the Church

1. William Samarin, *Tongues of Men and Angels: The Religious Language of Pentecostalism* (New York: MacMillan, 1972).
2. This is the rendering given the term by Anthony Thiselton,

The First Epistle to the Corinthians (Grand Rapids, Mich.: Eerdmans, 2000), 970.

3. Fee, *The First Epistle to the Corinthians*, 630-31; see also Richard B. Hays, *First Corinthians* (Louisville: John Knox, 1997), 223.

4. Christopher Forbes, *Prophecy and Inspired Speech in Early Christianity and Its Hellenistic Environment* (Peabody, Mass.: Hendrickson, 1997), 185-86. The fact that tongues are said to cease at the *parousia* (1 Cor. 13:8) leads Thiselton to conclude that it *cannot* be angelic speech, for why would a heavenly language terminate in the *eschaton* (see his *First Corinthians*, 973, 1061-62)? But it would not be heavenly speech per se that ends, but heavenly speech on the part of humans designed to compensate now for the limitations endemic to our fallen, preconsummate condition.

5. Grudem, *Systematic Theology*, 1072.

6. Jackie Pullinger's story may be found in her autobiography, *Chasing the Dragon* (Ann Arbor, Mich.: Servant Books, 1980).

7. Hayford, *Spiritual Language*, 40.

8. Stibbe, *Know Your Spiritual Gifts*, 179.

9. Jack Hayford, *A Passion for Fullness* (Dallas: Word, 1990), 31.

TEN
Letting Your Gift Find You

1. James I. Packer, *Keep in Step with the Spirit* (Old Tappan, N.J.: Fleming H. Revell, 1984), 249.

RECOMMENDED READING

The Beginner's Guide to Spiritual Gifts is just that, a *beginner's* guide. I hope you are now ready to dig more deeply into God's Word on this issue. Listed below are a few of the better books on the charismata.

Banister, Doug. *The Word and Power Church.* Grand Rapids, Mich.: Zondervan, 1999.

Carson, Donald A. *Showing the Spirit: A Theological Exposition of 1 Corinthians 12-14.* Grand Rapids, Mich.: Baker, 1987.

Deere, Jack. *Surprised by the Power of the Spirit.* Grand Rapids, Mich.: Zondervan, 1993.

_____. *Surprised by the Voice of God.* Grand Rapids, Mich.: Zondervan, 1996.

Fee, Gordon D. *God's Empowering Presence: The Holy Spirit in the Letters of Paul.* Peabody, Mass.: Hendrickson, 1994.

Forbes, Christopher. *Prophecy and Inspired Speech in Early Christianity and Its Hellenistic Environment.* Peabody, Mass.: Hendrickson, 1997.

Grieg, Gary S., and Kevin N. Springer. *The Kingdom and the Power: Are Healing and the Spiritual Gifts Used by Jesus and the Early Church Meant for the Church Today? A Biblical Look at How to Bring the Gospel to the World with Power.* Ventura, Calif.: Regal, 1993.

Grudem, Wayne, ed. *Are Miraculous Gifts for Today?: Four Views.* Grand Rapids, Mich.: Zondervan, 1996.

_____. *The Gift of Prophecy in the New Testament and Today.* Revised edition. Wheaton, Ill.: Crossway, 2000.

Keener, Craig S. *Gift & Giver: The Holy Spirit for Today.* Grand Rapids, Mich.: Baker Academic, 2001.

Kydd, Ronald. *Charismatic Gifts in the Early Church.* Peabody, Mass.: Hendrickson, 1984.

Lederle, Henry I. *Treasures Old and New: Interpretations of "Spirit-Baptism" in the Charismatic Renewal Movement.* Peabody, Mass.: Hendrickson, 1988.

Menzies, William W. and Robert P. Menzies. *Spirit and Power: Foundations of Pentecostal Experience.* Grand Rapids, Mich.: Zondervan, 2000.

Stibbe, Mark. *Know Your Spiritual Gifts: Practicing the Presents of God.* London: Marshall Pickering, 1997.

Turner, Max. *The Holy Spirit and Spiritual Gifts in the New Testament Church and Today.* Revised edition. Peabody, Mass.: Hendrickson, 1998.

White, John. *When the Spirit Comes With Power: Signs and Wonders Among God's People.* Downers Grove, Ill.: InterVarsity Press, 1988.

Wimber, John. *Power Evangelism.* San Francisco: Harper & Row, 1986.

Other Books in
The Beginner's Guide Series
Include:

The Beginner's Guide to Spiritual Warfare
by Neil T. Anderson and Timothy M. Warner

The Beginner's Guide to the Gift of Prophecy
by Jack Deere

The Beginner's Guide to Fasting
by Elmer Towns

The Beginner's Guide to Intercession
by Dutch Sheets

The Beginner's Guide to Receiving the Holy Spirit
by Quin Sherrer and Ruthanne Garlock

Ask for them at your nearest Christian bookstore or
go to **www.servantpub.com**